WORLD AIRLINE COLOURS

of Yesteryear

By: Ricky-Dene Halliday

London • England

Published by:
The Aviation Data Centre Ltd.
PO Box 92,
Feltham,
Middlesex, TW13 4SA,
England.

Telephone: 081 751 3317

Production and Print Management:
BennettDeBruin
No.2, The Grand Union Business Park,
Packet Boat Lane,
Cowley,
Middlesex, UB8 2GH,
England.

Telephone: 0895 846409

ISBN: 0 946141 50 9

INTRODUCTION

Welcome to World Airline Colours of Yesteryear, the latest in a series of Aviation Data Centre titles devoted to recording and detailing the liveries of the world's airlines - past and present.

The book primarily focuses on a ten year period, between the mid-'sixties and mid-'seventies, with coverage of 100 airlines - including many that are sadly with us no more. The illustrations have been carefully selected to capture the classic airliners of this period, with no less than forty different types covered. It is a collection of memories, a portfolio of quality photographs from the past, and whether you are a model maker, historian or purely an aviation enthusiast, I hope that you will enjoy reading and referring to this edition as much as I have enjoyed compiling it.

In addition to the acknowledgements that appear below, I would also like to thank my wife Elaine and daughter Rebecca for their endless patience during the long hours spent researching this title, and to Martin J. White for his part in making it all possible. Thanks also to Gary De Bruin and Paul Bennett for their involvement in the production of this book.

Ricky-Dene Halliday
October 1992.

Acknowledgements

Gunter Endres (World Airline Fleets 1977-1987), Tony Merton Jones (British Independent Airlines/Propliner), Brian Tomkins (Airlines & Airlines and Airliners), M. Wickstead and R. Cooper (European Dakotas), Tony Eastwood and John Roach (Piston Engine, Turboprop and Jet Airliner Production Lists), and Phil Lo Bao, Philip Eastwood and Alan Bushell.

Illustrations

Peter J. Cooper - Aer Lingus (B-707), Aeroflot (IL-62), Aerolineas Argentinas (B-707), Air Ceylon (DC-8), Aviaco (SE-210), Bangladesh Biman (B-707), British Caledonian (VC-10), BEA (Vanguard), BEA Airtours (Comet), BOAC (VC-10/B-707), Cambrian (1-11), Court Line (1-11/L.1011), East African Airways (DC-3), Egyptair (IL-62), Ghana Airways (VC-10), Iraqi Airways (B-707), KLM (DC-8), Malev (IL-18), Martinair (DC-9), National (B-747), PIA (B-707), Qantas (B-707), Spearair (DC-8), Swissair (Cv-990A), TAP (B-707), Turkish Airlines (DC-10), Wardair (B-707) and Zambia (HS-748); **Phil Lo Bao** - Cambrian (DC-3) and British Midland (Canadair C4); **Capt. John Lesch** - Eagle Airways (Viking), Cunard Eagle (Britannia) and Sabena (DC-6); **Ronald Herron** - BKS (Trident), British Island Airways (DC-3), British United Air Ferries (Carvair), Sabena (Cv-440) and SAS (DC-6/DC-7): **Mr. D. Stoner** - Aer Lingus (F-27) and Euravia (L-049); **Richard Vandervord** - British Air Ferries (Carvair - bottom); **Maurice Patrick** - British Air Ferries (Carvair - top); **Peter Keating Collection** - Aeroflot (IL-18/Tu-104), Aer Turas (Br.170/DC-4/DC-7/Britannia), Air Spain (Britannia/DC-8), Balair (DC-6), British United (VC-10), Dan Air (DC-7/1-11/B-707/Comet), CSA (IL-18), Flying Tigers (CL-44), Germanair (1-11), SAM (DC-6), Saturn (B-707), Seaboard World (DC-8), TAE (DC-7), Transavia (DC-6), TMA (DC-6), Trans Meridian (DC-7), UAT (DC-6), United Arab Airlines (IL-18) and UTA (DC-6); **Lockheed (via Henry Tenby)** - American Airlines (L.188), Eastern Air Lines (L-1049), Iberia (L-1049), KLM (L.188), South African Airways (L-749), TWA (L-1649), Varig (L-1049) and Western (L.188), **plus special thanks to Tony Eastwood**.

AER LINGUS

Aer Lingus Teoranta was formed on May 22nd 1936 with the assistance of Blackpool and West Coast Air Services and began operations, initially between Dublin and Blackpool, using a small fleet of de Havilland Rapides. The expansion of services across the Irish Sea gained momentum during the immediate post war period, due mainly to the availability of larger and faster aircraft such as the Douglas DC-3 and Vickers Viking. In 1947, Aerlinte Eireann was set up to provide services across the Atlantic, which finally commenced on April 28th 1958 using Lockheed Super Constellations (flown in association with Seaboard & Western Airlines) to New York and Boston. The operations of these airlines were fully integrated in 1960 and the airline became known as Aer Lingus - Irish International Airlines.

The company became the first airline in the world to operate the Fokker Friendship, taking delivery of eight aircraft between November 1958 and May '59 to supplement its existing fleet of Douglas DC-3s. The airline had earlier taken delivery of four Viscount 700s between March and April 1954 and three Viscount 800s from May 1957. Another three Viscount 800s joined the fleet at the beginning of 1959 and in early 1960 the series-700 aircraft were sold. The Viscount 800 fleet continued to grow and between 1960-1967 a total of eleven used examples were acquired, including nine from KLM, and these effectively replaced the Fokker F.27-100s which left the fleet in 1966. Cargo flights were initially the responsibility of a small fleet of Bristol Freighters.

Another milestone was reached in October 1960 when Aer Lingus became the first European airline to introduce the Boeing 720, which replaced Super Constellations on the transatlantic routes. In the years that followed the company continued to roll over and update its fleet, introducing ATL-98 Carvairs from February 1963, Boeing 707-320Cs from June 1964, BAC 1-11-200s from May 1965, Boeing 737-200s from March 1969 and 747-100s from December 1970. The Carvairs were used on car ferry operations connecting Dublin with Liverpool and Cork with Bristol, and during the summer months a seasonal Dublin-Cherbourg service was also operated. During their time with Aer Lingus the three Carvairs also assumed the airline's scheduled cargo network (flown mostly at night) to ensure maximum utilisation of the fleet. The car ferry services lost popularity once regular sea crossings had been established, and with Viscounts available for nocturnal freight hauling (following conversion) the hardworking Carvairs became surplus to requirements and were sold at the beginning of 1968. The last Viscounts had departed by 1971, leaving Aer Lingus with a modern all-jet fleet.

The livery illustrated by Boeing 707-320C EI-ANV was introduced by the first Super Constellations in 1958, which initially entered service with 'Aerlinte Eireann' titles. The titling was soon changed to read 'Irish Air Lines' and again in 1960 to 'Irish International Airlines', to reflect the new marketing name of 'Aer Lingus - Irish International Airlines'. The existing domestic and regional aircraft continued to use the livery illustrated by Fokker F.27-100 EI-APG until the mid-'sixties (the Friendships not being repainted until early 1965), although all new additions to the fleet adopted the new Irish International scheme, including the Boeing 720/707/737/747, Carvair, BAC 1-11 and all subsequent Viscount 800 aircraft. The green roof colouring was reinstated in later years as part of brighter and more fashionable design, which remains in use today.

IRISH AIR LINES
AER LINGUS · AERLINTE EIREANN

Aeroamerica was formed on January 7th 1974 and commenced operations from Boeing Field (Seattle) using a single Boeing 720, operating worldwide passenger and freight charters. A second aircraft was added in July of that year and between 1975 and 1976 several more 720s and some 707s were acquired. The airline established operational bases in Berlin and Cairo and specialised in operating services for other airlines from these stations. Clients included Saudia, Sudan Airways, Egyptair, Turk Kibris Hava Yollari, Somali Airlines and PIA. From Berlin, the airline also operated holiday charters to the Mediterranean and had scheduled route authority between Tempelhof and Saarbrucken.

By the summer of 1975 Aeroamerica was operating no fewer than seven Boeing 720s and two 707s. A BAC 1-11-400 was leased for the summer of 1976 to boost charter capacity from Tempelhof. The aircraft was repainted to wear an established two-tone orange design over the bare metal finish of American Airlines, which had previously operated the aircraft. Aeroamerica frequently made use of existing paint work and many of the liveries adopted, although extremely bright and colourful, had originated elsewhere. Two examples are given by Boeing 720s N730T and N736T, which share similar designs but different colouring. Another aircraft, N733T, had a white cheatline and motif set against an orange and mustard background, with titles reversed out of the cabin roof in white.

Contract work for other carriers started in 1976 when a Boeing 720 was operated on behalf of Egyptair, between September and December. The Egyptian carrier also leased a Boeing 707 from Aeroamerica over a period of eighteen months, between February 1976 and August 1977. During the following year as many as four aircraft were flying for other airlines simultaneously, but from 1978 these contracts started to dry up and rarely involved more than one aircraft at a time. At around the same time Aeroamerica added four early production Boeing 707s, retired one of its 720s and sold one of its original 707s. Two of the 'new' 707s were sold the following year and replaced by two ex-Pan Am 707-320Bs, which were to become the last aircraft to display Aeroamerica's name.

The remaining Boeing 720s withdrew to Seattle and with them went the colourful liveries that had been associated with the airline for so long. In its final days Aeroamerica used a stylised Eagle's head tail motif which also inspired new titling, but the exterior decor was generally neglected and its ageing fleet of Boeing 707s invariably looked tired and old. The airline was clearly experiencing some financial difficulties long before it finally ceased operations at the turn of the 'eighties.

AEROFLOT

Aeroflot was originally formed in March 1923 as Dobrolet and commenced operations that same year between Moscow and Ninji Novgorod (now Gorki), and southwards to Oral, Karkov, Kiev, Odessa, Batum and Tiflis, using small de Havilland, Junkers and Vickers aircraft. Services to and within Central Asia followed later, including a connection to Urga (Mongolia) and Kabul (Afghanistan). In 1929 Dobrolet became Dobroflot, when it absorbed the Ukrainian company Ukvozzduchput, which had opened a Kharkov-Kiev service on April 15th 1925 with a fleet of six Dornier Komets. After the merger of all civil aviation activities (except for Arctic services which were operated under the jurisdiction of Glawsewmorputj or Polar Aviation from 1933 to 1960), Dobroflot was reorganised in 1932 as Grazdansij Wozdusnyj Flot or Aeroflot. Limited external services were established during the following years but these had to be suspended in 1941, together with all internal services west of Moscow. After the war, Aeroflot concentrated on maintaining and developing its already vast domestic network, using mostly Lisunov Li-2s and later Ilyushin Il-12s and Il-14s. Air links were also established with other countries of similar ideology.

During the years that followed Aeroflot benefited enormously from the rivalry that developed between the Soviet design bureaus and their western counterparts, particularly in the race to put the first jet passenger aircraft into service. Shrouded by mystery and intrigue, the existence of the Soviet Union's first jet airliner (the Tupolev Tu-104) finally became known when the prototype aircraft brought General Serov to London Airport on March 22nd 1956, at a time when the British built Comet 1 had been grounded following a spate of accidents. Deliveries of production Tu-104s to Aeroflot began in May and the first domestic jet service (Moscow-Irkutsk) was opened on September 15th 1956. The 50-seat Tu-104 was purely an interim model, for in 1956 work was already in hand to produce the 70-seat Tu-104A, which in the autumn of 1957 set many international speed/height with payload records. Further developments included the 100-seat Tu-104B and the smaller 44 to 56-seat Tu-124, which entered service on Aeroflot's domestic network from April 1959 and October 1962 respectively. Other types added from 1959 included the Antonov An-10 (and the higher capacity An-10A), Ilyushin Il-18, Tupolev Tu-114 and, from October 1962, the Antonov An-24. The 75-seat Il-18 was intended for trunk and principle feeder services, and entered service with Aeroflot on April 20th 1959. From January 1960 the Il-18's network was extended to Sofia and Bucharest, and then to Cairo and East Germany, and before long all Eastern European capitals were served by the type. The Il-18 was also used extensively on Aeroflot's network to the Middle East, Africa and South East Asia for many years. Subsequent versions of the type included the 90 to 110-seat Il-18V and the longer range Il-18D, with greater fuel capacity. The Tupolev Tu-114 was derived from the Tu-95 bomber and entered service with Aeroflot on long range domestic and international services, seating 170 tourist-class passengers with a 48-seat restaurant cabin amidships. By far the world's largest commercial passenger aircraft at the time, the Tu-114 entered service with Aeroflot on April 24th 1961 on the 4,350 mile route from Moscow to Khabarovsk in eastern Siberia. Some two and half years later the type inaugurated a non-stop service to Cuba, bringing Havana within twenty hours flying time of the Russian capital; Montreal, Delhi, Conakry, Accra, Paris and Tokyo were also served by the fleet of thirty or so aircraft. While all this was going on Aeroflot's future fleet was already under development, with the Ilyushin Il-62 and Tupolev Tu-134 having completed their first flights in January and December 1963 respectively. These aircraft eventually entered service in 1967 and were later joined by the Tupolev Tu-154 from early 1972, and the wide-bodied Il-86 from December 1980. While Aeroflot may not have succeeded in introducing the supersonic Tupolev Tu-144 into passenger service as planned, its shortcomings in this field can easily be forgiven considering some of the purpose built freighters that did enter service over the years, such as the Antonov An-22 and An-124, which took the world by storm.

AEROFLOT

The featured liveries are just a small selection of those used by Aeroflot up until the fleetwide introduction of the present design from 1975, until which most aircraft retained their original delivery schemes. Aeroflot's Il-18 fleet carried the same colour scheme for eighteen years (illustrated by CCCP-75440), and as late as the mid-seventies some of the earlier Tupolev jets could still be seen in the vintage livery illustrated by Tu-104B CCCP-42459. It is thought that prior to 1975 the design and application of Aeroflot markings was left to the manufacturer, which could explain why the Tu-134 and Il-62 entered service during the same year but in totally different liveries. Furthermore, the Tupolev design was later adopted by the Tu-154 while the Il-62's livery (illustrated by CCCP-86650) was applied to the first Il-76s. After 1975 all new aircraft were delivered in a standard Aeroflot livery while the earlier types, with the exception of the An-22s, were either repainted or phased out.

AEROLINEAS ARGENTINAS

Aerolineas Argentinas was formed as a State corporation in May 1949 when the Ministry of Transport took over the activities of all airlines with the exception of the Air Force-controlled LADE. The companies involved in the merger were Flota Aerea Mercantile Argentina (FAMA), which operated international services to the United States and Europe; Aeroposta Argentina, dating from 1928; the flying boat operator Aviacion del Litorial Fluvial Argentino (ALFA) and Zones Oueste y Norte de Aerolineas Argentina (ZONDA).

Aerolineas Argentinas introduced four Boeing 707-320Bs during the winter of 1966/67 to replace Comet 4Bs used on long haul routes. These were later supplemented by two 707-320Cs delivered a year or so later, and by two purchased from World Airways in 1971. The Boeing 707s were gradually relegated to secondary routes as wide-bodied Boeing 747s, introduced from December 1976, became the long haul flagships.

The livery illustrated by Boeing 707-320B LV-ISA, seen landing at London-Heathrow in July 1974, had been used by all jet aircraft operated up until this time, including Comet 4s delivered to the airline from February 1959 and Boeing 737-200s introduced at the start of the seventies. The design was eventually changed in November 1974 for that which is in use today.

AER TURAS

Aer Turas Teo (Gaelic for Aer Tours Ltd.) originally commenced operations in the summer of 1962 as an air-taxi company company using a de Havilland DH.89 Rapide bi-plane. Initially, Aer Turas relied on ad-hoc business, consisting mostly of small group charters around Ireland or to the United Kingdom, coupled with pleasure flying on fine summer weekends from Dublin Airport. In April 1964 the Rapide was replaced by a 28-seat Douglas DC-3, and throughout the summer this was operated on passenger and freight charters to the UK and continental Europe. It was then decided to re-organise Aer Turas as a larger, more versatile charter operator using a Douglas DC-4, which it was felt would overcome the low winter passenger traffic problem by virtue of its good cargo capacity. The DC-3 was returned to the UK in the autumn of 1964 and the business of re-organising the company went ahead throughout the winter. An Air France night mail DC-4 became available and was purchased early in 1965. The aircraft was delivered from Toulouse to Dublin in June 1965, and Aer Turas was back in business. With its 72 seats or eight-tonne cargo capacity the DC-4 found a lively market on both long and short haul work. Much of that first summer's business came from a contract awarded by Cambrian to fly scheduled passenger services out of Liverpool. Ship's crew charters, frozen meat contracts and general cargo work became the norm after the summer had died away, and the aircraft was soon seen in such places as Gibraltar and Hong Kong. Regular inclusive-tour and student charter contracts were flown out of Dublin for the 1966 season, thus ensuring a busy summer for the DC-4. A decision was then taken which was later to have a very profound effect upon the airline's future - to enter the bloodstock transportation business. A Bristol 170 Mk.31 was eventually acquired for this purpose, joining the company's fleet in March 1966. The airline later won a major contract from Aer Lingus to operate freight schedules to London, Liverpool, Manchester and Birmingham, which took effect from November 1st 1966. In order to provide better flexibility and stand-by back-up, a second Bristol Freighter was acquired later that month. The fleet was depleted with the loss of this aircraft in a landing accident at Dublin in June 1967, but the following month saw the delivery of a second Douglas DC-4 to take its place. This aircraft, which was in a non-convertible cargo configuration, went on lease to Alitalia in the autumn of 1967 for six months, during which time it was repainted with Alitalia titles and tail markings.

The summer of 1967 also marked the virtual end of passenger flying for Aer Turas, the original DC-4 having been used on student charters to Madrid and Munich and on inclusive-tour services to Barcelona. The DC-4 was now becoming uncompetitive for this kind of work by virtue of its low speed, so it was decided to concentrate on cargo charters. During 1968 two further subcontracts were undertaken, one involving the operation of passenger services in Africa for Air Mauritanie and the other for Transport Flug of West Germany, flying a daily Lufthansa cargo service from Manchester to Frankfurt. Bloodstock work was at this stage developing rapidly and later in 1968 the company secured the major part of the bloodstock agency contracts. This meant Aer Turas now had a virtual monopoly of this business between Ireland, the UK and France, which provided a long term, lucrative base to its operation.

Further expansion was now being contemplated and the decision was taken to enter the specialist long-haul market with Douglas DC-7 equipment. The airline finalised a package deal with KLM involving the purchase of four DC-7CFs at the beginning of 1969. Two of these were sold in Gabon shortly afterwards, and operations with the two remaining aircraft - appropriately registered EI-ATT and 'ATU - commenced in May 1969. Aer Turas subsequently disposed of its two Douglas DC-4s which meant the bulk of its bloodstock operation was undertaken by the Bristol 170. This arrangement proved unsuccessful and later that year the airline purchased another DC-4 and released one of the DC-7s for sale. In March 1971 Aer Turas undertook an evaluation of the Argosy, using a Series-100 aircraft chartered from Nittler Air Transport. Following this it was decided to replace the remaining DC-7 with the type, and a three year lease contract was signed with Transair Canada for the lease of an Argosy 222, which entered service in November of that year. 1972 was to be a difficult year for the airline as the Argosy, although well suited to the short-haul bloodstock work, was unable to secure much ad-hoc business owing to range/payload restrictions. By June the situation was critical, so the Argosy was grounded and attempts were made to terminate the lease. The aircraft was later used to operate a high frequency shuttle carrying flowers from Jersey to Bournemouth during a dock strike, but nevertheless an agreement was reached with Transair for the return of the Argosy in September. After that traumatic event the airline was completely reorganised, and it was decided to sell the Bristol Freighter and replace the Argosy with a Douglas DC-7.

The decision to return to a DC-7 operation was prompted by the need to have an aircraft of Argosy-sized payload (ie: about 14 to 15 tonnes) capable of undertaking non-stop flights to Greece or North Africa, where there was evidence of an emerging requirement for livestock work. A suitable DC-7CF was located in Miami and was put into service in December 1972. A second DC-7, actually a smaller DC-7BF, was purchased in May 1973, being intended originally as a back up from September onwards. The good results of the latter part of 1973 led Aer Turas to consider further expansion. The DC-7 was being severely hampered by the dwindling availability of 115/145 grade fuel necessary for obtaining optimum payload/range performance, thus virtually precluding the aircraft from any long haul work. Consequently, it was decided to replace the DC-7s with a turboprop type and the choice was soon narrowed down to the Bristol Britannia, which combined good payload/range performance with high reliability and low acquisition cost. Monarch Airlines was offering an attractive package which embraced crew training, maintenance and part-financing, so it was decided in February 1974 to proceed with the purchase of one of these aircraft, which duly arrived at Dublin on May 24th 1974. The DC-7BF had been retired in December 1973, and the introduction of the Britannia became even more urgent following the loss of DC-7CF EI-AWG at Luton Airport on March 3rd The Britannia soon proved itself an ideal aircraft for Aer Turas and the fleet was later standardised on the type. The remaining Douglas DC-4 was eventually sold in April 1977, by which time Aer Turas had two Britannias in full-time operation, later joined by a third aircraft on lease. Turboprop operations passed to the Canadair CL-44 in later years and finally came to an end in May 1989, when Aer Turas established an all-jet fleet based on the Douglas DC-8-63CF, which had been in use since October 1982.

The livery illustrated by Bristol 170 EI-APC was originally introduced by Douglas DC-4 EI-AOR in June 1965, although both aircraft were repainted between October/November 1966 to wear a new green, white and red design. Douglas DC-7s EI-ATT (illustrated) and EI-ATU made use of the previous KLM livery, overpainted in yellow and green. Douglas DC-4 EI-ARS also adopted this scheme initially but following overhaul in September 1972 was repainted to wear the design illustrated, which also welcomed DC-7CF EI-AWG to the fleet. The final featured livery was synonymous to the Britannia fleet, illustrated in its original form by EI-BAA.

AER TURAS–IRISH INDEPENDENT AIRLINES

AIR ALGERIE

Air Algerie was founded in 1946 as a non-scheduled carrier under the title of Compagnie Generale de Transport Aeriens (C.G.T.A.). A regular network was gradually developed, which included services to Paris, Marseille and Toulouse, and consolidated following the merger with Compagnie Air Transport in April 1953, when the present name was adopted. Services were operated within Algeria and to numerous destinations in France. By 1965 the airline's stock was divided mainly between the Government (57%) and Air France (28%), with the fleet consisting of three Douglas DC-3s, ten Douglas DC-4s and five Caravelles. Air Algerie had been an early customer for the Caravelle, taking delivery of three series-1/1A aircraft during the winter of 1959/60. These were later converted to Caravelle 111 standard and joined by two Caravelle 6Ns during the summer of 1961. Major expansion took place from the start of the 1970's as Boeing 727-200s and 737-200s began to supplement the Caravelles on international services. The domestic fleet was also modernised with the introduction of turboprop Convair 640s (from late 1968) and Nord 262As (during the winter of 1970/71). A new livery was introduced and in 1972 Air Algerie became wholly Government owned. As more Boeing jets were delivered so the airline's network spread throughout Africa and Europe.

Leading up to the permanent use of wide bodied aircraft on its heavily travelled Algiers-Paris route, Air Algerie often leased other aircraft to provide extra capacity. Among the types to wear the airline's full red and white livery were Boeing 707s of British Midland (G-AZJM illustrated), an Airbus A300B1 of Trans European Airways and a Boeing 747-200C of World Airways.

AIR CEYLON

Originally founded as Ceylon Airways, the airline began operations on December 10th 1947 with a service from Colombo to Madras in India. In the following year the name was changed to Air Ceylon Ltd. and the network was further extended to Singapore and London. In 1951 the airline was made an independent corporation with the Government holding 51% of the stock and Australian National Airways holding 49%. A route to Australia was also opened.

The Australia-Ceylon-London services were abandoned in 1953, but in co-operation with KLM a route to Europe was re-opened in 1956. The services were again suspended in October 1961 and the agreement with KLM terminated. Services to London and Singapore were resumed in April 1962 using Comets chartered from BOAC. On the domestic front, a modest fleet of Douglas DC-3s provided connections within Ceylon and also crossed the Gulf of Maanar to Madras in southern India. Direct services to Bombay were inaugurated following the introduction of an Avro 748 in October 1964. The regional network was enhanced by the arrival of a new Hawker Siddeley Trident 1E in July 1969, which opened up many new routes and introduced jet speed and comfort to the existing sectors. The Trident's network eventually linked Colombo with Delhi, Madras, Bombay, Karachi, Bangkok, Kuala Lumpur and Singapore.

In early 1972 the airline entered into an agreement with UTA and a Douglas DC-8-53 was leased from the French carrier for use on services to London and Paris. In 1977 Air Ceylon purchased a DC-8-43 from Air Canada and also leased a Boeing 720 from Templewood Aviation, by which time Sharjah had been added to its network and a second Avro 748 had been acquired. Air Ceylon later ceased operations, which led to the formation of Air Lanka on September 1st 1979.

Air Charter International was formed on February 7th 1966 as a wholly-owned charter subsidiary of Air France, and began operations using aircraft loaned from its parent soon afterwards. In 1970 the airline purchased its own fleet of Caravelle 111s from Air France (F-BJTG illustrated) and these were joined in 1972 by two ex-PSA Boeing 727-200s, which had been acquired to perform non-stop flights from Paris to the Canary Islands and the southern tip of Morocco with a full payload.

The Caravelles entered service in September 1970 wearing the basic colouring of Air France but with Air Charter titles and tail markings. This application was taken a step further with the introduction of the Boeing 727s in 1971 (as illustrated by F-BPJU), but none of the Caravelles were repainted to wear this livery and many years passed before the two types shared a common image. By this time Air Charter had introduced a completely new colour scheme and the original Air France Caravelle 111s had been retired. Following in the footsteps of Air France, Air Charter adopted white overall fuselage colouring and for many years combined this with large 'ACI' titles. The original red, white and blue tail motif was phased out with the introduction of a subsequent livery, which remains in use today. Later models of the Caravelle were used until 1990 in collaboration with Europe Aero Service, while Air Charter's fleet grew with the transfer of Boeing 727, 737 and Airbus A300B4 equipment from Air France.

The airline's long standing relationship with the Caravelle finally came to an end on October 27th 1990 when a Caravelle 10B, operated on Air Charter's behalf by Europe Aero Service, flew the return leg of Bordeaux-Tenerife IT charter.

AIR FRANCE

Air France was established on August 30th 1933 when SCELA (Societe Centrale pour l'Exploration de Lignes Aeriennes), itself formed on May 17th 1933 by an amalgamation of Air Orient, Air Union, CIDNA and SGTA, purchased the assets of Compagnie Aeropostale, which had built up its reputation through its pioneering work across the South Atlantic. Air France continued to expand the operations of its predecessors and quickly established itself as one of the world's leading airlines. Soon after the war a new company, Societe National Air France, was formed (on January 1st 1946) which rapidly rebuilt the pre-war European network as well as introducing services across the North and South Atlantic on June 25th. Societe National Air France was superseded on September 1st by a reconstituted Compagnie Nationale Air France.

Air France took delivery of four Lockheed L-049 Constellations and 15 Douglas DC-4s during the summer of 1946, which together with DC-3s and Languedocs formed the nucleus of its fleet. Its association with the Constellation was to last well into the sixties as the company continued to re-equip with newer and larger models, taking delivery of twenty-four L-749s between 1947 and 1951, ten L-1049Cs in 1953, fourteen L-1049Gs between 1955 and 1957 and finally ten L-1649 Starliners between 1957 and 1958. Many of the DC-4s delivered to Air France in 1946 were still earning their keep as freighters at the start of the 'seventies. A more unusual type employed by Air France was the Breguet 763 Provence, of which twelve were operated by the airline on its Sahara routes from 1952, with six later being converted for cargo use.

The company's long association with the Caravelle began on May 6th 1959 with the type's inaugural service from Paris to Istanbul, and by December 1960 some twenty-four were on line. Altogether, a total of fifty Caravelles were operated by the airline, and proved difficult to replace in later years. Air France took delivery of seventeen Boeing 707-328s between November 1959 and October 1960, which started to replace the Constellations and Starliners on transcontinental services and relegate them to high-density short to medium-haul routes and charter flights. The Boeing 707 fleet grew steadily year by year and by 1968 a total of thirty-eight aircraft had been delivered, including eight -320Bs and nine -320Cs. Some of the latter models were reconfigured for all-cargo use, supplemented by three ex-Pan Am aircraft acquired between September 1975 and April 1976.

Another type that entered service in the late sixties was the Boeing 727-200, initially with four aircraft joining the fleet between March and May 1968, followed by a further fifteen between 1969 and 1972. Later joined by nine Advanced models, the 727 played a significant role with the airline over a period spanning more than twenty years.

The original post war livery of Air France was to remain in use for some thirty years, albeit with some minor adjustments along the way. In its earlier form the cheatline originated below the forward window line as a continuation of the company's motif, and the separation of these represented the only significant change to the design. In later years a lighter blue was adopted and the tail insignia became sharper. This revision was introduced by the first Airbus Industrie A300Bs in 1974 and was adopted by many of the newer types, including two 737-200s operated in the French West Indies. However, despite all these refinements the company eventually realised that the time had come to modernise its image and the livery illustrated overleaf slowly disappeared with the Caravelles.

Air India International Ltd. was established on March 8th 1948 by Air India Ltd. (formerly Tata Air Lines), which provided 51% of the capital, and the Indian Government with a 49% holding. Operations commenced on June 8th 1948 with a weekly Bombay-London service, via Basra, Cairo and Geneva. Known as the 'Route of the Magic Carpet' it was flown by three Lockheed L-749 Constellations delivered earlier that year. Air India became a wholly State-owned corporation on August 1st 1953 and was designated the country's international flag carrier following the nationalisation of all air transport in India. The original L-749s were soon replaced by a fleet Super Constellations from April 1954, which were later sold to the Indian Air Force following the delivery of six Rolls Royce Conway-powered Boeing 707-420s between February 1960 and April 1962. By 1965 the airline's network reached Paris, Geneva, Moscow, Prague, Frankfurt, Rome, Nairobi, Aden, Karachi, Tokyo, Bangkok, Hong Kong, Singapore, Perth and Sydney. In addition a service to Kuwait from Bombay was flown using VC-10s chartered from BOAC.

Air India added five Boeing 707-320B/Cs at a rate of one a year from 1964, and from April 1971 Boeing 747-200B 'flying palaces' were introduced on the Bombay-London-New York route. The Boeing 747s were named after Indian emperors and had 'palace arch' surrounds to their windows. None of the earlier 707s were repainted to wear this scheme, despite the fact that many of the Pratt & Whitney-powered aircraft remained in use until 1988. The newer livery was, however, adopted by the regional fleet of Airbus A300s and A310s in later years.

Air Inter was formed in 1954 and commenced operations on March 17th 1958 over a network linking the cities of Paris, Strasbourg, Lyons, Nice, Marseille, Toulouse, Lordes/Tarbes, Bordeaux and Nantes. Major expansion followed with the introduction of Viscount 700 equipment from October 1961, which formed the mainstay of domestic operations for many years to come. Initially receiving seven from Air France, the airline continued to acquire aircraft from other sources up until 1966, by which time a total of fifteen had adopted its livery. Another type used by Air Inter was the Nord 262B, which first entered service with the airline on July 24th 1964. Four of these 29-seat aircraft were acquired for use on lower density routes, leaving the Viscounts to concentrate on more densely travelled sectors. However, the Nord 262s were sold to Rousseau Aviation in the winter of 1968 as a new relationship with the Fokker Friendship began to blossom.

Jet operations were started in 1966 when the airline introduced two Caravelle 111s to its network (F-BNKB illustrated), which were quickly followed by ten more aircraft. Four ex-Air France Caravelles were later acquired and in 1972 Air Inter received the first of five Caravelle 12 aircraft it had on order. The airline eventually operated twelve Caravelle 12s following the purchase of seven from Sterling of Denmark between 1980 and 1983. Air Inter also supported the development of the Dassault Mercure, taking delivery of ten of these aircraft from April 1974, later joined by a modified pre-production model. In more recent times the airline has re-equipped with Airbus A300s and A320s, although the Friendships and Mercures still play an active role.

AIR SPAIN

Air Spain was formed in May 1966 and commenced operations later that year using the first of two Bristol Britannia 312 aircraft to be acquired from British Eagle. Much of that first winter was dedicated to crew training and familiarisation in preparation for the busy summer season ahead, with a full programme of holiday charter flights scheduled to begin with the arrival of a third aircraft (ex-El Al) at the beginning of May. However, some ad-hoc charters were undertaken and in March 1967 the airline initiated a weekly IT charter between Palma and Birmingham. The use of turboprop equipment played a major part in the initial success of Air Spain, at a time when most Spanish charter airlines were equipped with older piston-engined airliners such as the Douglas DC-4 and DC-7. The aircraft was capable of operating IT charters with full loads from Helsinki to both the Balearic and Canary Islands, without the need for refuelling.

As the first summer season came to an end Air Spain was forced to chase new opportunities to keep its fleet active during the off-peak winter months, and discovered a valuable source of income transporting tomatos from the Spanish mainland (Alicante) and Canary Islands (Las Palmas) to the United Kingdom (Liverpool, Manston and Gatwick) and Germany. This work eventually outgrew the size of the fleet and the airline occasionally found itself having to lease additional capacity to keep pace with demand. In December 1969 Air Spain purchased a dedicated Britannia 312F freighter from ex-British Eagle stocks to ease this pressure, and to provide year round support for its growing involvement in this field. On the passenger front, Air Spain's Britannia fleet (EC-BFL illustrated) had been ferrying holidaymakers to Palma, Ibiza, Valencia, Barcelona, Seville, Gerona and Malaga from points such as Birmingham, Gatwick, Luton, Belfast, Dusseldorf, Basle, Geneva, Brussels, Rotterdam and Helsinki. Services were later operated to the Caribbean (including Cuba), while regular freight flights also served Ostend.

By the turn of the seventies the company was looking to make the transition to jet aircraft, which it achieved through the purchase of six DC-8-21s from Eastern Airlines between 1971 and 1973. The first aircraft arrived in January 1971 and initially supplemented the existing Britannia fleet. One of the Britannias (the freighter) was sold towards the end of the year to make way for a second DC-8 and as more of these aircraft were delivered between 1972 and 1973 so the remaining Britannias were phased out. The DC-8-21 fleet was later reduced by the sale of one aircraft to Aerovias Quisqueyana in February 1974, by which time the company was said to have been experiencing some financial difficulties.

Air Spain's transition to jet aircraft also coincided with the introduction of a completely new livery, as illustrated by DC-8-21 EC-BZQ. None of the Britannias were repainted and for a while the airline operated both types in different schemes. Air Spain eventually ceased operations in February 1975 when rising costs, coupled with the poor economics of its fuel thirsty DC-8 fleet, made it difficult for the airline to compete in a market it had once dominated.

AIR MALAWI

Air Malawi was formed on September 1st 1967 to succeed another company of the same name, which had been established in March 1964 as a subsidiary of Central African Airways Corporation to take over local services in the newly independent state of Malawi, formerly known as Nyasaland. The 'new' airline assumed the domestic and regional network of its predecessor and commenced operations using two Viscounts, a Douglas DC-3 and a Beech Baron. Among the points served from Blantyre's Chileka Intl. Airport were Johannesburg, Lusaka, N'dola, Nairobi, Salisbury and Beira.

The original fleet was eventually rolled over and replaced by two Hawker Siddeley (Avro) 748s, two Britten-Norman Islanders and two BAC One-Elevens. On December 3rd 1974 the airline inaugurated a weekly service between Blantyre and London (Gatwick) using an ex-British Caledonian Vickers VC-10. The eleven and a half hour flight included a technical stop at Nairobi and was flown by Air Malawi until October 29th 1979, when the VC-10 was placed into store at Bournemouth-Hurn pending disposal. During its operational career with the airline it was also used on regional services to Johannesburg and the Seychelles, with these routes later passing to the BAC 1-11 fleet. A long haul service to Colombo (Sri Lanka) was also inaugurated by the VC-10 in November 1976.

The livery illustrated by VC-10 YQ-YKH is very similar to that which in use today, although nowadays the wedged cheatline is less profound and the titles appear somewhat smaller.

ALIA - THE ROYAL JORDANIAN AIRLINE

Alia was formed in December 1963 to replace Jordan Airways, which itself had succeeded Air Jordan of the Holy Land two years earlier. The new airline, named after King Hussein's daughter, commenced operations on December 15th between Amman, Jerusalem, Beirut, Cairo and Kuwait using two ex-Royal Jordanian Air Force Handley Page Heralds. These were soon joined by two Douglas DC-7s during the summer of 1964 and the network was expanded.

On June 7th 1965 the airline signed for a new Caravelle 10R and took delivery of this a month later, when operations with the smaller Herald came to end. A second Caravelle was ordered later that year and before long these aircraft were flying to London, Frankfurt, Paris, Rome and Athens, as well as regionally to Tehran and Kuwait. The two Douglas DC-7s were lost on June 5th 1967 and a third Caravelle was ordered to replace them. In 1971 two Boeing 707-320Cs were delivered, and the Caravelles were relegated to secondary services such as Amman-Beirut. Ironically this trip took four hours flying time, because Syria had closed its airspace to Jordanian aircraft and the Caravelles had to fly south to the Red Sea, then north to Cairo and finally off the Israeli coast into Lebanon. Eventually a couple of ex-Pan American Boeing 720Bs and some new 727-200s were added and the Caravelles were sold by April 1975.

The livery illustrated by Boeing 707-320B JY-AEB was introduced in January 1971 and remained the standard colouring of Alia until the first TriStar 500s were delivered from September 1981, after which many new colour schemes were evaluated. In addition to the Boeing 707s, it was also adopted by 720B, 727 and 747-200C aircraft, the latter introduced from April 1977.

ALITALIA (& SOCIETA AEREA MEDITERRANEA)

Alitalia was originally formed on September 16th 1946 in association with British European Airways, under the title of Aerolinee Italiane Internazionali (Alitalia), and commenced operations on May 5th 1947 - initially between Rome, Naples, Catania and Turin. International services were introduced in 1948 and initially served Tripoli, Cairo, Lisbon, Paris, Nice, Geneva, London and Buenos Aires, and by the end of 1949 a network spanning 12,925 route miles had been established. In the spring of 1950 the airline acquired four ex-Pan American Douglas DC-4s to replace its original fleet of Avro Lancastrians and SIAI-Marchetti S.M.95s, and a route to Caracas was opened in July of that year.

The present name was adopted on September 1st 1957 when the airline amalgamated with Linee Aeree Italiani (LAI), which had been founded on the same day as Alitalia but with financial and technical support provided by Trans World Airlines (TWA). Following a period of re-organisation the fleet was strengthened by the arrival of Convair 340s and Douglas DC-6s from 1953. The Convairs were later modified to -440 standard and remained in use until 1961. The airline inherited a fleet of five DC-6s, twelve DC-3s and six Viscount 700s from LAI , and introduced Douglas DC-7s on long haul routes from the winter of 1957. The Viscount 700 fleet was expanded in later years with the addition of both new and used aircraft, and remained active until 1970.

Alitalia ordered four Caravelle 3s on October 15th 1959 and inaugurated services with the type on June 13th 1960. The four aircraft were later converted to Series 6N standard and by the summer of 1967 a total of twenty-one Caravelle 6Ns were employed. Alitalia also took delivery of fifteen DC-8-43s (I-DIWA illustrated) between 1960 and 1965 and the DC-6 and DC-7 fleets were gradually phased out, with some of these passing to Alitalia's charter subsidiary - Societa Aerea Mediterranea (SAM). This airline, originally formed in 1928, was re-organised by Alitalia as a non-IATA charter and IT operator in November 1960. Scheduled freight services were also undertaken on the national carrier's behalf, serving Frankfurt and Tripoli from Rome, using two Curtiss C-46F Commandos. Passenger operations were upgraded to jet equipment from 1968 following the introduction of two former Alitalia Caravelles. The national carrier was able to release more of these aircraft as Douglas DC-9-32 deliveries progressed, which enabled SAM to dispose of its remaining Douglas DC-6s. In 1974 it was decided that the airline should be merged into Alitalia and operations continued until 1977, when Societa Aerea Mediterranea finally ceased to exist. In the meantime Alitalia had re-equipped its short-haul fleet with Douglas DC-9-32s and introduced DC-8-62s, Boeing 747-100/200Bs and DC-10-30s to its medium and long haul networks. As part of this fleet renewal process the Caravelles and DC-8-43s were phased out during the mid-seventies. Alitalia also acquired a fleet of eighteen Boeing 727-200s from October 1976, although these were replaced by McDonnell Douglas MD-80s in later years.

The original livery of Societa Aerea Mediterranea is illustrated by Douglas DC-6B I-DIMU. The full green, white and red tail colouring was adopted by the Caravelle fleet and in later years the current Alitalia scheme was used, together with black 'SAM' titling. Alitalia's livery was changed prior to the introduction of Boeing 747-100s on the Rome-New York route in June 1970.

AMERICAN AIRLINES

American Airlines was organised on May 13th 1934 as a direct successor to American Airways Inc., which was formed on January 25th 1930 to consolidate the services of numerous predecessor companies dating back to 1926. The oldest of these, Robertson Aircraft Corporation, had inaugurated the first regular scheduled air mail service between Chicago and St. Louis with a de Havilland DH.4 flown by Charles Lindbergh. American extended its transcontinental routes with the purchase of Standard Air Lines (October 1930) and Century Pacific Lines (1932), and entered the international field in 1946, when it opened services to Mexico City from El Paso and Dallas. The airline also made important contributions to the development of such designs as the Douglas DC-3, DC-7, Convair 240 and 990, Lockheed Electra and, as recently as 1968, the McDonnell Douglas DC-10.

The livery illustrated by Lockheed L.188A Electra N6101A 'Flagship New York' welcomed the type to American's fleet in November 1958. This was a very significant time in the history of the airline as it marked the transition to both turboprop and jet equipment by American, the first Boeing 707-120s having been delivered a month earlier. The use of highly polished metal was not uncommon during the previous piston era, but in applying this to the next generation of airliners it became something of a company trademark. In later years the cheatline was shortened to taper at the nose, the red outlining disappeared from the titles and the eagle motif was moved to the fin. This revision was made with the introduction of Boeing 727-100 and BAC 1-11-400 aircraft from the mid 'sixties and provided the basis for the design now in use today.

AUTAIR

Autair was originally formed in 1953 as a London-based helicopter company and began airline operations during the summer of 1960 using the first of three Douglas DC-3s to be acquired from British European Airways, initially operating passenger and freight contract and charter flights. This work continued through 1962 when the airline added two Vikings to supplement its growing involvement in the IT market. This was given a further boost in 1963 when the airline acquired three Airspeed Ambassadors from Globe Air of Switzerland (via Handley Page). The Ambassadors (G-ALZZ illustrated) were completely refurbished, at a cost of around £6,000-00 each, prior to entering service with the airline from October 1963.

On September 27th 1963 the airline changed its name to Autair International Airways and scheduled services were inaugurated four days later (on October 1st), initially between Luton and Blackpool, using the Vikings. The scheduled network was expanded with services connecting Hull with Luton and Jersey, and in 1965 the two Vikings were replaced by two Avro 748s on these routes. Further expansion coincided with the arrival of three Handley Page Heralds in 1966, and by the following year Teeside, Hull, Blackpool, Carlisle and Glasgow were all reached from Luton, with the Isle of Man and Amsterdam served during the summer months.

BAC 1-11-400s replaced Ambassadors during the summer of 1968 when Autair's IT activities reached new heights. Further 1-11s were added to the fleet and the scheduled operations were gradually wound down. On January 1st 1970 Autair officially changed its name to Court Line and concentrated solely on IT work.

AVIACO

Aviaco was formed by a group of businessmen in the industrial town of Bilbao in 1948, initially to fly perishable goods with a small fleet of Bristol Freighters. Passenger operations followed with the introduction of regular services connecting Bilbao with Madrid and Barcelona in 1950. These routes were progressively expanded to supplement the network of the national carrier, Iberia. This relationship was strengthened in 1954 when Iberia, together with its parent - the Institute de Industria (INI), acquired a majority shareholding in the airline. The move helped to regulate the issue of traffic rights and gave Aviaco financial aid in acquiring a fleet of Convair 440s from Sabena. By 1965 the airline was operating six Convair 440s, five Douglas DC-4s and two Carvairs, the latter on vehicle ferry operations between Palma, Majorca, Barcelona and Valencia. Its range of services also included seasonal IT charters to the United Kingdom. During 1970 the INI gave fresh consideration to the role of Aviaco, ensuring autonomy for the airline and setting specific targets, especially in the charter field. These plans were implemented in April 1971 and the results of the restructuring can be gauged from the 1972 passenger figure of 241,000, compared with 88,500 the year before. Aviaco acquired six Caravelle 10Rs from Iberia in 1972 and five -6Rs the following year. The aircraft were introduced on the airline's domestic and international network, and were also extensively used for charter flights, later supplemented by Douglas DC-8s.

The livery illustrated by Caravelle 6R EC-ATX took Aviaco into the jet age and was also adopted by DC-8, DC-9-30 and Fokker F-27 aircraft operated thereafter. On June 27th 1974 the colouring of this design was changed to blue and white, a combination that had been used in earlier years.

BALAIR

Balair was formed in 1948, initially as a flying school, and commenced charter operations five years later when Swissair acquired a financial interest in the company. Subsequently, many of the aircraft operated by the airline were supplied by Swissair, including Douglas DC-4s from 1959 and Douglas DC-6Bs from 1961 - which together with Fokker Friendships formed the nucleus of the fleet during the 'sixties. In addition to the usual range of passenger and freight charters, Balair also specialised in relief and support operations under contract to the United Nations and International Red Cross organisations. During the Biafran airlift in 1969 the airline operated four ex-USAF Boeing C-97s and a C-160 Transall on behalf of the Intl. Red Cross, and also commited two of its own Douglas DC-6s to the cause, one of which was lost in Biafra in January of that year. By 1970 the fleet consisted of one Douglas DC-3 (operated exclusively for the United Nations in the Middle East), one DC-4 (sold during that year), three DC-6s and four Fokker Friendships (later phased out during the winter of 1971/72). A Douglas DC-8-55F freighter was added in April 1971 as Balair began to re-shape its fleet, later joined by a DC-8-63PF in May of the following year. Nevertheless, one of the Douglas DC-6s remained in operation and was still flying passenger and cargo services for Balair up until the summer of 1982!

The livery illustrated by Douglas DC-6B HB-IBZ, photographed at Geneva-Cointrin in June 1969, was carried by all type's operated by the airline, later including a DC-8-62CF and a DC-9-30 (from April and November 1976 respectively), and a DC-10-30 (from January 1979).

Balkan Bulgarian Airlines can trace its history back to 1947 and the formation of the Government-owned Bulgarshe Vazdusne Sobstenie (BVS), which had provided a small local network and a service to Prague (via Belgrade) from July of that year. After a period of two years the airline was reformed as a joint Bulgarian-Soviet undertaking and the name TABSO was adopted. The new airline began services with a fleet of Lisunov Li-2s, supplied by the Soviet Union, and in 1954 became wholly Bulgarian-owned when Russia's 50% holding reverted to the Government. From 1956 the Li-2s were supplemented by a small fleet of Ilyushin Il-14s, but it was not until the introduction of Il-18s from 1962 that TABSO was really in a position to expand its international network from Sofia. The airline took full advantage of the increased range offered by these turboprop airliners and opened a succession of new routes to western Europe, Africa and the Middle East as the fleet grew in strength. On the domestic and regional front the piston-engined Li-2s and Il-14s were gradually replaced by Antonov An-24s, introduced from 1966, which have remained in use ever since - supplemented by Yakovlev Yak-40s in later years.

In 1968 a separate charter subsidiary was formed to satisfy the growth in inclusive tour traffic to the Black Sea resorts of Varna and Burgas. Known as Bulair, the airline also assumed responsibility for cargo charters and acquired two Antonov An-12s for this purpose, while passenger operations were conducted by a fleet of six Il-18s supplied by TABSO. The name Balkan Bulgarian Airlines was also adopted in 1968 and with it came a new red and white livery to coincide with the introduction of Tupolev Tu-134 equipment from September of that year. During this transitional period the Il-18s displayed a variety of liveries based on the previous pale blue colouring of TABSO, some with 'Bulgarian Air Transport' titles and secondary Bulair markings (illustrated by LZ-BER) and others with 'Bulair' titles and motifs (illustrated by LZ-BEM). This situation improved when Bulair was reintegrated with the parent company in 1972, and these aircraft were subsequently repainted to wear a common Balkan livery. The original red and white design was retained by some domestic and Government/VIP aircraft while the An-24s, Il-18s, An-12s, Tu-134s and Tu-154s (introduced from 1972) adopted revised green and red colouring. This livery was also carried by some of the remaining Il-14s and by an Antonov An-30 survey aircraft.

The name TABSO was created from the initials of the original Soviet-Bulgarian Air Transport partnership and has featured in all subsequent liveries, despite the dissolution of this agreement in 1954. The shortened 'Bulgarian Air Transport' titles reflected this change in ownership but the airline was still officially known as TABSO until the present identity was adopted in 1968. The TABSO motif was incorporated within the tail colouring of initial Balkan liveries and can be found alongside the titles of the modern design in use today.

BANGLADESH BIMAN

Bangladesh Biman was created on January 4th 1972 as the new national airline of the State of Bangladesh, formerly East Pakistan. The new carrier began operations a month later with scheduled services from Dacca to Chittagong, Sylhet and Jessore, using a Douglas DC-3 loaned from the Bangladesh Air Force. The airline later acquired two Fokker Friendships from Indian Airlines, and also received a gift of two each from the Netherlands and Australian Governments. In June 1973 a Boeing 707-320 was leased from Templewood Aviation and regular scheduled services to London (Heathrow) followed. Bangladesh Biman purchased its own Boeing 707-320C six months later and the leased aircraft was returned. Further examples of the 707-320C were acquired as the airline expanded its international network, while two Fokker Fellowships were later added for regional expansion.

Boeing 707-320 S2-ABM illustrates the original pale blue livery of Bangladesh Biman, as worn by the first Fokker F-27s, with titles appearing in Bengali in this starboard view. The airline took the opportunity to modify this with the introduction of Boeing 707-320C S2-ABN on December 28th 1973, darkening the shade of blue used in the cheatline colouring and extending this over the upper rear fuselage to encompass the fin. This design was still in use when the airline took delivery of its two Fokker Fellowships in late 1981, but had been changed prior to the introduction of the first McDonnell Douglas DC-10-30s in August 1983, when the national colours of green and red were adopted.

BRANIFF INTERNATIONAL AIRWAYS

Braniff Airways was organised on November 3rd 1930 from an earlier company, Braniff Airlines, which had been founded on June 20th 1928 by the brothers Paul and Tom Braniff. A scheduled service was opened on November 13th 1930 between Tulsa, Oklahoma City and Wichita Falls and extended to Kansas City, St. Louis and Chicago a year later. Two small carriers, Long and Harmon Airlines and Bowen Air Lines were absorbed on January 1st 1935, and on August 15th 1952 Braniff further increased its by then considerable network with the acquisition of Mid-Continent Airlines. MCA had been formed as Tri-State Airlines and apart from its regional routes in the central states operated important through-connections from the Canadian border as far south as New Orleans and Houston. The name Braniff International Airways was adopted in 1948 when new services were opened to Havana and Lima. The take-over of Pan American-Grace Airways (Panagra), which had initiated services on May 17th 1929, added further valuable routes and cities in South America to Braniff's network from February 1967.

Braniff made the transition to jet and turboprop equipment at the close of the 'fifties in an effort to replace earlier piston-engined aircraft such as the Douglas DC-6 and DC-7 ahead of its competitors. The airline ordered ten Lockheed L.188A Electras for delivery from April 1959 and four Boeing 707-220s, introduced between December 1959 and February 1960. These were joined by five Boeing 720s from February 1961, but a replacement for the smaller piston-engined Convair 340/440 aircraft was still needed. This was met by the purchase of fourteen BAC 1-11-200s which Braniff placed into service in April 1965, ahead of Mohawk and American Airlines. When the first 1-11 was delivered in March of that year Braniff employed a fleet of seventeen Cv-340/440s, five Douglas DC-7Cs, eleven Douglas DC-6s, nine Electras, four 707-220s, and six 720s (including one acquired from Aer Lingus). Later that year the airline signed for twelve Boeing 727-100s for delivery from May 1966, and also placed its first order for the 707-320C. Braniff received nine of these aircraft between May 1966 and November 1967 and although they helped to replace the remaining Douglas DC-7Cs their usefulness was relatively short lived. The Boeing 727 order was more significant as the type later dominated domestic operations, the fleet eventually being standardised on the larger Series -200 model. A fleet of Douglas DC-8-30s was inherited from Panagra in February 1967 but were replaced by seven DC-8-62s (originally ordered by Panagra) between August and December of that year. Braniff later signed for two DC-8-62s for delivery in late 1969, and in 1973 four DC-8-51s were purchased from National Airlines. During the early 'seventies the earlier Boeing 707/720s and BAC 1-11s were phased-out and sold, with the Electras having already left the fleet by March 1969. Even the newer 707-320Cs were leased-out or sold between 1971/72 as the fleet became standardised on Boeing 727 and Douglas DC-8 equipment, the latter for use on longer range domestic routes and the network into Latin America. An order for two Boeing 747-100s was later reduced to just one aircraft, which entered service on the daily Dallas Ft.Worth-Honolulu service on January 15th 1971. The '747 fleet was increased several years later when Braniff extended its network to Europe, with the addition of three new 747SPs and some used Series-100/200B aircraft.

The origin of the colourful liveries associated with Braniff can be traced back to April 1965 and the appointment of Harding L. Lawrence as the airline's new chairman. Up until then the airline's image was based on patriotic red, white and blue colouring, although the 'Fly Braniff' schemes adopted from 1959 were certainly far from appealing. Lawrence joined Braniff from Continental Airlines, where he had been instrumental in creating the 'golden jet' image, and firmly believed that bright and interesting colour schemes enhanced passenger appeal. Taking this further than ever before, he elected to paint different aircraft in different colours - originally seven, and later nine, pastel shades - using an all-over scheme with white fin, wings and horizontal stabiliser. In 1971, coinciding with a fleet rationalisation, the variety was reduced to four two-tone colour schemes (orange/mustard, red/tan, green/olive and dark and pale blue) with the upper colour continuing through the fin and with bare metal wings and stabiliser (as illustrated by Boeing 720 N7076). The Boeing 747 displayed its own unique livery based on the previous design but with the fuselage and 'BI' motif painted orange (as shown). Later, in 1973 and 1975 respectively, Douglas DC-8-62 N1805 and Boeing 727-291 N408BN were repainted to wear special abstract liveries designed by artist Alexander Calder. The Douglas DC-8 (illustrated) was the most brightly coloured of the two as it represented the 'Flying Colors of South America'. The theme for the '727 was 'The Flying Colors of the United States' and so it was therefore painted red, white and blue. As a further development, all Braniff aircraft carried the legend 'Flying Colors' alongside the 'BI' motif. By 1978 several aircraft had been repainted to wear a new livery which introduced burgundy to the existing colour range as part of a completely re-styled design. With this, the familiar 'BI' motif disappeared from the fleet and five years later Braniff also ceased to exist, for the time being anyway!

BI

BKS AIR TRANSPORT

BKS Air Transport came into existence in October 1951, taking its name from the initials of its three founders - messrs Barnby, Keegan and Stevens. The airline initially operated a single Douglas DC-3 on ad-hoc and contract charters from its Southend base. In 1953 BKS established another centre of operations at Newcastle and inaugurated scheduled services connecting West Hartlepool with Northolt and Newcastle with Jersey and the Isle of Man. Inclusive tour services were also being flown from Newcastle, in addition to Southend, by which time the airline was operating a fleet of five Douglas DC-3s. Services from Leeds began in 1955 and by then several Vikings were supplementing the DC-3s on IT work. These in turn were replaced by Ambassadors in 1957. In 1960 the company launched a vehicle ferry service from Liverpool to Dublin, although this operation was short lived.

BKS introduced its first turboprop equipment in 1961 in the form of a Viscount 700 leased from Maitland Brewery Aviation. From 1962 the airline began to build up a fleet of Avro 748s, chiefly for operation on its trunk route between Leeds and London. 1964 saw a big step forward with the introduction of Britannia 102 aircraft (G-APLL illustrated), which operated scheduled services from Newcastle to London and onwards to various French and Spanish destinations. The Britannias were employed on IT flights, relegating a reduced fleet of Ambassadors to all-cargo work. By 1969 the DC-3s, Ambassadors, Bristol 170s and Avro 748s had all been retired, with the fleet having been standardised on Viscount and Britannia aircraft. However, the four Britannias were also reaching the end of their operational careers with BKS and in the spring of 1969 the airline introduced two Trident 1Es to replace them.

In 1964 British European Airways had purchased a 30% holding in BKS and in 1967 both Cambrian and BKS became fully owned by BEA through a holding company called British Air Services. In 1970 BKS changed its name to Northeast Airlines to reflect its regional identity, and the story continues with this airline (see page 104)

40

British Air Ferries, known until October 1967 as British United Air Ferries, was formed in January 1963 through the merger of Channel Air Bridge (founded in 1959) and Silver City Airways. Both companies specialised in cross-channel vehicle and passenger services, Silver City having inaugurated the world's first car ferry service on July 14th 1948.

With the advent of roll on/roll off sea ferries BAF found its car trade declining and it was progressively forced to trim its routes and frequencies. In October 1970 Freighter G-ANWM operated the last vehicle ferry flight from Lydd to Le Touquet, and early in 1971 the axe fell on the Lydd-Ostend route too. Operations now focused on Southend, home of the Carvairs, which were now starting to haul freight instead of the vehicle/passenger combinations they had been designed for. British Air Ferries continued to operate passenger services to Ostend and Le Touquet from Southend using leased Viscounts and HS-748s.

In October 1971 Mr. T.D. Keegan purchased the company from Air Holdings and began to implement major expansion plans. Efforts were made, without success, to fly scheduled passenger/cargo services to the Channel Islands from Coventry and Bournemouth (using the Carvairs), while Canadair CL-44s were actually introduced on some Southend-Ostend schedules. These aircraft were also used on services to Basle and Rotterdam, having been acquired via Trans Meridian Air Cargo - another of Mr. Keegan's companies! CL-44 operations were found to be hopelessly uneconomic and the type withdrew from BAF service in 1972.

Carvairs continued to fly the passenger services to Ostend and Rotterdam until they were replaced by Heralds in early 1975. After that Carvair operations were scaled down, with the type being finally withdrawn in 1976. In the years that followed British Air Ferries acquired a large fleet of Viscounts, the majority from British Airways, to supplement its Heralds. The company developed its aircraft leasing business, specialising in oil related contracts both at home and abroad. Inclusive tour services were introduced from Southend to the Channel Islands and contract work for other airlines and freight forwarding companies provided more work for the fleet as scheduled operations were gradually wound down.

The livery illustrated by Carvair G-ASHZ was used to change the previous blue and mustard colouring of British United, a new image being created simply by repainting the existing cheatlines in two tone blue and changing the tail initials from BUA to BAF. In later years dark blue undersides were added as evident in a splendid scene at Southend Airport during the summer of 1974, and later still some of the remaining Carvairs adopted a completely re-designed scheme which featured diagonal gold and blue bands over the fuselage and fin. British Air Ferries also characterised its Carvairs by giving them names such as 'Porky Pete', 'Big Louie', 'Big Joe', 'Big John', 'Big Bill' and 'Fat Albert'. The names 'Plain Jane' and 'Fat Annie' were adopted by two Carvairs that were stripped of paint and operated as freighters in later years.

BRITISH CALEDONIAN AIRWAYS (BCAL)

British Caledonian Airways was created on November 30th 1970 when Caledonian Airways, which had initiated non-scheduled passenger and cargo operations on November 29th 1961, merged with British United Airways. The new airline was initially known as Caledonian/BUA, with the name British Caledonian Airways being adopted on September 1st 1972.

At the time of the merger both airlines were involved in inclusive tour charter flying, although British United had also developed a scheduled network which included routes to East and Central Africa, South America, and to various points in Europe. Caledonian's plans to operate scheduled services to the United States had been opposed, although group affinity charters were undertaken to the USA, Canada, the Far East and Australasia. The operations of the two airlines therefore complimented each other, and with a combined fleet of three VC-10s, seven Boeing 707-320Cs, two Bristol Britannias (phased out by May 1971), eight BAC 1-11-200s and twelve BAC 1-11-500s, the airline was ready and equipped for major expansion. Following the report of the Edwards Commitee on British Civil Aviation and the formation of BCAL the new airline was awarded the British flag services to West Africa and to Libya and licensed to operate regular scheduled services between London and Paris. However, the airline had to wait several years before it could cross the North Atlantic with similar authority.

The basic livery illustrated by VC-10 G-ASIX was adopted by all types operated by British Caledonian, later including McDonnell Douglas DC-10-30s, Boeing 747s and Airbus Industrie A310-200s. The airline effectively ceased to exist on April 14th 1988 following a merger with British Airways, although its name and motif was retained for charter operations.

BRITISH ISLAND AIRWAYS

In November 1962 the passenger networks of Silver City Airways and Jersey Airlines were merged to form British United (Channel Islands) Airways, as part of the Air Holdings Group. The airline's name was subsequently changed to British United Island Airways in 1968 and then, on July 20th 1970, to British Island Airways. From 1962 onwards the company operated a fleet of Douglas DC-3s, Herons, Heralds and Viscounts on routes to the Isle of Man and Channel Islands.

By the time the name BIA was adopted the Viscounts and Herons had departed, and so had all but three of the Dakotas. They were used chiefly on freight services and were finally retired in May 1974. After that BIA's fleet was standardised on the Herald, with sixteen of these aircraft serving with BUIA/BIA - although not at any one time. The busiest routes were from Southampton and Gatwick to the Channel Islands and from Blackpool to the Isle of Man. Some international routes were also operated, for example to Dublin, Paris and Amsterdam.

British Island Airways joined forces with Air Wales and Air Anglia to form Air UK on January 16th 1980, by which time the airline was also operating a fleet of BAC 1-11s on inclusive tour services from Gatwick. Douglas DC-3 G-AMSV illustrates the original red and white scheme of British Island Airways at Guernsey in the early seventies.

BRITISH EAGLE (EAGLE AIRWAYS/CUNARD EAGLE)

This company began operations as Eagle Aviation in April 1948, initially operating a fleet of Halifax freighters on the Berlin Air Lift. In 1949/50 these aircraft were replaced by Avro Yorks with Eagle operating these on worldwide passenger and freight charters. Throughout the 1950s the airline progressively expanded its operations with the introduction of Douglas DC-3s and Vickers Vikings. Scheduled operations were inaugurated in June 1953 with a regular service between Blackbushe and Belgrade, with inclusive tour charters being introduced at around the same time.

By 1958 the airline's scheduled network had been expanded to cover a variety of European destinations from Blackbushe, including Dinard, Innsbruck, Luxembourg and Ostend. Services were also being flown from Manchester and Birmingham and the fleet now featured Viscount 700s and Vikings, with the DC-3s and Yorks having been phased out. In 1958 a subsidiary airline, Eagle Airways (Bermuda), began flying Viscounts from Bermuda to New York and later Miami. To cater for longer range charters and Air Ministry trooping flights Eagle purchased several Douglas DC-6s between 1958 and 1961. A new red, white and black livery was also introduced but not before the airline's first DC-6 had been delivered in the livery illustrated by Viking G-AMGI.

In March 1960 the Cunard Steamship Company acquired a controlling interest in the company and the trading name Cunard Eagle Airways was adopted. At the same time the airline began to operate Bristol Britannia aircraft (G-ARKB illustrated) and in 1961 one of these was used to inaugurate scheduled transatlantic services from London to Miami, via Bermuda and Nassau. By now the airline was operating from London Heathrow, with Blackbushe having been closed to commercial traffic at the beginning of 1960.

Cunard applied to operate domestic, European and transatlantic routes in competition with BEA and BOAC in the early 'sixties, though very few of these were granted. It did, however, continue to build up its Viscount and Britannia fleets and phased out its remaining Vikings by 1962. The airline had also purchased two Boeing 707s in the hope of successfully gaining a license to operate them from London to New York. These plans did not materialise although one of the '707s was used on the London-Bermuda-Nassau-Miami schedule. In 1962 Cunard gave up hope of even being able to mount a transatlantic service in competition with BOAC and so it formed a new company with the Corporation, BOAC-Cunard, to fly these routes, and sold its interest in Eagle Airways shortly afterwards. Following this, the airline changed its name (in October 1963) to British Eagle International Airways.

Again the airline applied for licenses in competition with BEA, this time more successfully. In 1963 British Eagle inaugurated scheduled services connecting London (Heathrow) with Edinburgh, Glasgow and Belfast. Further expansion followed later that year when the company acquired Starways and its network of scheduled services from Liverpool. Between 1964 and 1966 British Eagle continued to find employment for its fleet of Britannias and Viscounts on inclusive tour charters, Government contracts, ad-hoc charters and scheduled services. A small fleet of BAC 1-11s, introduced in 1966, replaced Britannias on scheduled domestic trunk routes.

In 1968 the airline purchased three Boeing 707s to operate transatlantic charters and hopefully scheduled services as well. However, these were hard and difficult times for the industry and British Eagle was sadly to become a victim of this economic crisis, announcing the cessation of operations on November 6th of that year. The airline's final service was the arrival of Britannia G-AOVM at Heathrow on November 7th, bringing a cargo of oranges from Israel.

BRITISH EUROPEAN AIRWAYS (BEA)

British European Airways began life in February 1946 as the European division of British Overseas Airways Corporation (BOAC) and commenced operations on August 1st of that year. It was charged with the provision of all European and domestic scheduled services and operated from a base at Northolt. European services were initially flown with ex-BOAC Dakotas, and then by Vickers Vikings. The Vikings became the mainstay of its operations until 1952 when they were gradually phased out and replaced by the Airspeed Ambassador (Elizabethan), and later the highly successful turboprop Vickers Viscount.

BEA's route network quickly developed to incorporate most European capital cities and holiday destinations by the early 1960's. On the domestic front BEA inherited a variety of aircraft from the companies it took over in 1947. These included the Douglas DC-3, de Havilland Rapides, Junkers Ju-52s and Avro 19s. Domestic services were soon standardised on the Douglas and de Havilland types and between 1950 and 1952 the airline converted most of its DC-3s to Pionair standard, with built-in air stairs, updated flight deck and 32 passenger seats. Some DC-3s operated as Pionair/Leopard freighters and for a short time two were re-engined with Dart turboprops for familiarisation prior to the introduction of the Viscounts. The Dakotas were eventually replaced by Viscounts and Heralds in 1962. The Rapides remained in use until 1964, although by then they only operated the route from Lands End to the Isles of Scilly, which became the responsibility of a fleet of Sikorsky S.61 helicopters. BEA had operated a helicopter unit since 1947 and used S.51, WS.55 and Bristol 171 helicopters in a number of experimental roles, including the operation of scheduled passenger, mail and freight services.

At the end of 1960 BEA began introducing the 135-seat Vickers Vanguard, which it employed on high density domestic and European routes. Between 1969 and 1973 nine of these were converted to Merchantman freighters and replaced the Argosy, which BEA had been using on freight routes since 1961.

BEA entered the jet age in late 1959, introducing a fleet of Comet 4Bs on some of its longer routes as well as on mainline services such as London-Paris. A long association with the Hawker Siddeley Trident commenced in 1964 with the introduction of the Trident 1C. These were later joined by the longer range Trident 2s from 1968, which replaced the Comets, and by the higher capacity Trident 3s from 1971. In 1968 BEA also began to take delivery of eighteen BAC 1-11-500 aircraft. In 1972 the Government instigated a full merger between BEA and BOAC to form British Airways, and this legally took effect on April 1st 1974, ending BEA's existence.

The livery illustrated by Handley Page Herald G-APWC took BEA into the jet era and was adopted by all type's operated from late 1959, with the exception of the Douglas DC-3s and Rapides (the Elizabethans having been phased out during the previous year). This was replaced in 1969 by the design illustrated by Vanguard G-APER, which disappeared years ahead of it time following the formation of British Airways in 1974. One of the most interesting applications of this livery involved a Lockheed TriStar of Eastern Air Lines, which was repainted to wear the tail colouring and titles of BEA for its appearance at the 1972 Farnborough Air Show. The scheme was also used to welcome the Trident 3 to BEA's fleet, and with additional 'cargo' titles the Merchantman freighter as well. Variations of both designs were also adopted by the airline's helicopter division.

BEA AIRTOURS

BEA Airtours was formed on April 24th 1969 as a subsidiary of British European Airways to operate inclusive tour charters from Gatwick and Manchester. Equipped with a fleet of ex-BEA Comet 4Bs, the airline commenced operations on March 5th 1970 with a flight between Gatwick and Palma, this being one of several holiday destinations served regularly by the airline from that day onwards.

A fleet of nine Comet 4Bs were replaced by a similar number of ex-BOAC Boeing 707-436s from December 1971, with the type finally bowing out of service at the end of the 1973 summer season. The entire Comet fleet was acquired by Dan Air, together with a large spares inventory, with whom they served for many years after.

The livery adopted by BEA Airtours was identical to that of its parent, but with titles amended accordingly. On April 1st 1974 the airline became known as British Airtours, by which time it was flying to the Canary Islands, Tunisia, Morocco and the usual range of Mediterranean holiday destinations.

BRITISH AIRTOURS

When the Government decided to bring BEA and BOAC into a common management and eventually a total merger, the name British Airtours was adopted for BEA's Airtours subsidiary. This name was introduced in April 1974, by which time the airline was equipped with a sizeable fleet of Boeing 707-436s, acquired from BOAC.

In addition to the network inherited from BEA Airtours, British Airtours also operated inclusive tour flights to the United States and Canada as well as some round-the-world services. Capacity was also leased to other carriers, eg: Syrian Arab Airlines, while some BA flights used British Airtours aircraft too. By the end of the seventies nine Boeing 707s were in use, although due to the age of these aircraft coupled with rising fuel costs the airline was planning their retirement.

The Rolls Royce Conway-powered '707s finally bowed out in 1980 and were replaced by an assortment of Boeing 737s and Lockheed TriStars. A Boeing 747-200 was also used on select long haul IT charters crossing the Atlantic. As for British Airtours, following the merger of British Airways and British Caledonian in 1987 it was decided that the Caledonian name and motif should be preserved at the expense of BA's self-styled charter division, and so the company effectively ceased to exist.

BRITISH OVERSEAS AIRWAYS CORPORATION (BOAC)

British Overseas Airways Corporation was officially established on November 24th 1939 as a state owned airline to take over the routes of Imperial Airways and British Airways, and began operations on April 1st 1940. During the war it maintained services over a wide area of the world using Douglas DC-3s, various flying boats, B-24 Liberators and other fixed wing aircraft. In 1945 the Government decided it should provide intercontinental services while a new corporation - British European Airways - would assume the European and domestic routes. A third corporation, British South American Airways, was also set up to serve South America, although it was absorbed into BOAC in July 1949. Revenue operations began on April 1st 1946, and the corporation was responsible for all British flag services to the United States, Middle East and Commonwealth.

BOAC's worldwide network was developed using Avro York, Lockheed L-049/749 Constellation, Boeing Stratocruiser, Handley Page Hermes and Canadair C-4 Argonaut aircraft. Until November 1950 the corporation also flew flying boats such as the Boeing 314 and Short Solent. BOAC made history on May 2nd 1952 when it operated the world's first scheduled passenger service with a jet aircraft, namely the Comet 1. However, its experience with the type was not a happy one, and the fleet had to be withdrawn in 1954 following the break up of two aircraft in flight. The cause was eventually traced to metal fatigue in the pressurised hull. BOAC also ran into difficulties with its order for the turboprop Bristol Britannia, which it intended to use to replace the older piston engined aircraft. Severe development problems with the Britannia significantly delayed its introduction and a fleet of Douglas DC-7s had to be purchased as a stop gap measure. The Britannia finally entered service with BOAC in 1957, closely followed in 1958 by the Comet 4.

BOAC again made aviation history by opening the first commercial transatlantic jet service on October 4th 1958, using the Comet 4. A round-the-world jet service was inaugurated in 1960, and a Comet service to New Zealand on April 2nd 1963. BOAC was also instrumental in establishing and assisting many other airlines, particularly within the Commonwealth, and associated carriers included Aden Airways, Air Jamaica, Bahamas Airways, BWIA, Cathay Pacific, East African Airways, Fiji Airways, Gulf Aviation, Malaysian Airways and Nigeria Airways.

In 1964 the Corporation introduced the very popular VC-10 aircraft on its African/Far East routes, followed in 1965 by the Super VC-10 on the Atlantic services. The VC-10s replaced the Britannias and Comets and became the mainstay of BOAC operations for several years, although they were supplemented by a fleet of Rolls Royce Conway-powered Boeing 707-420s, which had been delivered from April 1960. In 1966 BOAC placed an order for six of the giant Boeing 747s and these subsequently entered service in 1970. As the '747 fleet was built up so VC-10 and Boeing 707 operations were scaled down. On the cargo front BOAC had operated a variety of aircraft, including the Douglas DC-7C and Canadair CL-44. By 1970 cargo operations were conducted with a small fleet of 707-320C freighters but the cargo carrying capacity of the '747s eventually made these redundant. BOAC was looking at the BAC/Aerospatiale supersonic Concorde by the early 'seventies, although an order for six of these magnificent aircraft did not come until 1976. By then BOAC and BEA had been merged to form British Airways, with the last day of BOAC's legal existence being March 31st 1974.

The familiar 'speedbird' motif has been displayed by all types operated by the airline and continues to play a role, albeit more subtle, in the current British Airways design. In the immediate post war years the motif, together with B.O.A.C. initials, was featured on the forward fuselage with the Union flag taking pride of place on the fin. However, following the introduction of new types such as the Hermes, Argonaut and Stratocruiser from 1948/49 the scheme was modified to include a blue cheatline, trimmed with gold, above which the cabin roof and tail was painted white. At this point the airline decided to relocate the titling to the upper mid fuselage and place the 'speedbird' motif at the top of the fin, alongside a scaled down Union flag. The registration letters were also moved to the fin where they became sandwiched between two horizontal blue bands. An example of this livery is given by Lockheed L-1049D N6503C, an aircraft leased from Seaboard & Western Airlines for a period of twelve months from March 1955. This arrangement

BRITISH OVERSEAS AIRWAYS CORPORATION (BOAC)

was reversed in 1957 in order to make the blue colouring more profound, prior to the introduction of the Douglas DC-7, Britannia 312, Comet 4 and Boeing 707-420 aircraft. This variation, illustrated by Britannia G-AOVH at San Francisco in June 1958, was also adopted by the Stratocruiser, Argonaut and Britannia 102 fleets, and applied to a Canadair CL-44 leased from Seaboard World between September 1963 and October 1965.

The next livery change was timed to welcome the first standard VC-10s to the fleet in 1964 and saw the horizontal fin bands replaced by an enlarged 'speedbird' motif, the Union flag moved to the lower forward fuselage, the registration incorporated within the cheatline (Boeing 707) or on the upper tail assembly (VC-10), and the forward cheatline arrangement expanded to incorporate B.O.A.C. titles. The colouring of the titles and motifs etc. was also changed from white to gold, and the gold coloured trim of earlier years was extended above the cheatline as well. This revised livery was adopted only by the VC-10s and Boeing 707s as the Comet 4s and Britannia 312s were to be phased out in 1965 and all other types had already left the fleet. Another variation of this scheme featured joint B.O.A.C.- Cunard titles.

BOAC-Cunard was formed in June 1962 to take over a large part of the western hemisphere operations of BOAC, and all the western hemisphere operations of Cunard Eagle Airways and its Bermudian and Bahamian subsidiaries. Created as a joint venture between the Cunard Shipping Company (30%) and BOAC (70%), BOAC-Cunard operated scheduled services between London and New York, Boston, Detroit, Chicago and Miami, and between Manchester, Glasgow and New York. It also operated from London to Bermuda, Nassau, Jamaica, Barbados, Trinidad, Lima, Caracas and Bogota, and provided services from New York to Bermuda, Nassau, Jamaica, Antigua, Barbados and Port of Spain on charter to BWIA. Equipment and staff were provided by BOAC.

In later years the cheatline was altered to sweep more evenly over the forward fuselage, the gold trim was dropped and the Union flag relocated above the cheatline, while more profound BOAC titles replaced the delicate B.O.A.C. application previously used. This livery, illustrated by VC-10 G-ARVJ, was also adopted by the first Boeing 747s, introduced from April 1970, although on these aircraft the titles were displayed on the raised cabin section (in blue). The fleet was eventually repainted to wear the original red, white and blue colouring of British Airways, although the livery of BOAC lingered for some time in the hybrid form illustrated by Boeing 707-320C G-AXGW.

BRITISH MIDLAND AIRWAYS

British Midland Airways can trace its history back to October 1938 when Captain Roy Harben established Air Schools at Burnaston, Derby's newly opened airfield. In 1949 the decision was taken to expand into commercial charter operations and a new company, Derby Aviation, was registered for that purpose. A single De Havilland Rapide was obtained, although other aircraft was also 'borrowed' on occasions.

Derby Aviation found plenty of work for its aircraft, particularly in charters to the Channel Islands and the Isle of Man. In July 1953 the company inaugurated scheduled services between Derby and Jersey, and to cope with the volume of traffic it purchased the first of many Douglas DC-3s. By 1959 eight Dakotas were flying schedules to the Channel Islands from Derby, Birmingham, Cambridge, Staverton, Luton, Oxford and Northampton. Rapides continued in service on some routes, particularly from Nottingham and Wolverhampton to Jersey, until 1957, when they were replaced by a small fleet of Miles Marathons

In 1958 the airline became known as Derby Airways and its DC-3s began flying inclusive tour services. A scheduled connection between Derby and Glasgow was also opened in 1958, serviced by the Marathons. In 1961 Derby Airways purchased three Canadair Argonauts (G-ALHG illustrated in early BMA markings) for its inclusive tour work, although the type also flew the Jersey schedule when additional capacity was required.

The name British Midland Airways was adopted on July 30th 1964 to reflect its regional identity and its move to the newly completed East Midlands Airport. By 1965 the company had obtained a Dart Herald, but loads soon outgrew the capacity offered by this potential DC-3 replacement and the airline focused its attention on the Vickers Viscount instead, introducing the type to its fleet from 1967. The Argonauts were retired in 1967 and the Dakota finally bowed out in 1969.

In 1970 the airline purchased three BAC 1-11 aircraft and a Boeing 707-320. The 1-11s were used on inclusive tour work and the '707 on Group Affinity transatlantic charters. The 1-11's career with the airline was short lived, with the three being sold in 1973 and the airline withdrawing from IT work for several years to come. The Boeing 707 fleet, however, was gradually expanded even though transatlantic charters ceased in 1972. British Midland used these aircraft between 1972 and 1984 for its 'instant airline' concept. Basically, an airline could charter one or more of these aircraft, which would be painted in its colours and supported by BMA staff. This concept was a huge success and consequently the '707 fleet was rarely seen in BMA's own colours.

The Viscount fleet was at the centre of all scheduled operations for a number of years, increasing in size as the network grew. The airline also renewed its association with the Dart Herald in March/April 1973 and later built up a sizeable fleet of Fokker Friendships, which the airline operated from 1981. Douglas DC-9-10s supplemented the Viscounts on domestic trunk routes from August 1976, and a major network of schedules with hubs at East Midlands, Birmingham, London (Heathrow) and Jersey was in operation by the start of the eighties.

The livery illustrated by Viscount 800 G-BFZL was carried by all type's operated by the airline until the introduction of the current design in October 1985, including BAC 1-11, Boeing 707, Dart Herald, Friendship, DC-9-10 and later Shorts 330/360 aircraft. The Viscount is the only type to have carried three different British Midland liveries, having been continually operated by airline from 1967 to 1988.

BRITISH UNITED AIR FERRIES

British United Air Ferries was formed in January 1963 following a merger between Channel Air Bridge and Silver City Airways, prior to which both companies had been purchased by the British United Group and managed by Air Holdings. The activity of BUAF focused on the provision of cross Channel vehicle ferry services from bases at Lydd and Southend. A smaller base was also maintained at Bournemouth (Southampton after 1966) to provide similar services to the Channel Islands.

The main equipment used was the Bristol 170 Mk.32 Super Freighter, although a number of Mk.21 and 31 Freighters were also flown. The company also operated the Aviation Traders Carvair, a Douglas DC-4 conversion, although these were chiefly flown from Southend. The most intensive schedules were flown from Lydd to Le Touquet in France. The company sought to operate some vehicle ferry services further into Europe, eg: to Basle and Geneva, and also tried to fly some services from Coventry and Manchester for the benefit of northern motorists. In October 1967 British United Air Ferries became known simply as British Air Ferries, reflecting its complete operational separation from British United.

Carvair G-ARSD is seen wearing the original livery of British United Air Ferries at Geneva in August 1965, with a now vintage Rover car about to be taken aboard. This was also the standard livery of British United Airlines and with minor adjustments, primarily to the tail colouring, was carried by several aircraft types during the sixties, including VC-10s and BAC 1-11s. The blue and mustard livery of BUA, illustrated by VC-10 G-ATDJ, was also adopted by the Carvairs in later years.

BRITISH UNITED AIRWAYS (BUA)

British United Airways was formed by the merger of Airwork and Hunting Clan on July 1st 1960 and inherited a mixed fleet of Viscounts, Britannias, Douglas DC-3s, DC-4s and DC-6s. Scheduled passenger services were operated to West, Central and East Africa, and also to Gibraltar, Rotterdam, Le Touquet and the Channel Islands, from a base at Gatwick. Some of the services to Africa were flown as 'Skycoach' services, providing lower fares than other scheduled flights. Other work undertaken included trooping flights to British bases as far afield as Singapore and Hong Kong, inclusive-tour charter services, and the operation of a scheduled freight service from London (Heathrow) to Central Africa.

In May 1961 BUA ordered ten BAC 111-200 aircraft to replace the Viscounts and allow it to expand its network, and they began to enter service from 1965. BUA also ordered two BAC VC-10s for its African services and these came on line in 1964. However, at that time BUA also took over the BOAC routes to South America and a third VC-10 was obtained to provide sufficient capacity. The One Elevens enabled the airline to offer a highly competitive service and in 1965/66 it began operating from Gatwick to Glasgow, Edinburgh and Belfast in competition with BEA's services from Heathrow. They also proved very popular with tour companies and BUA's IT programme expanded considerably. So successful was BUA's experience with the One Eleven that it purchased the longer series -500 aircraft, which began to be delivered in 1969. By then the Britannias, Viscounts, DC-4s and DC-6s had been retired. In 1970 some talks took place regarding a possible merger between BOAC and BUA, but eventually BUA and Caledonian Airways merged in November 1970 to create British Caledonian Airways.

CAMBRIAN AIRWAYS

Cambrian Airways was founded in April 1935 using a single De Havilland Gipsy Moth on light charter work in South Wales. Operations were suspended for the duration of the war but recommenced in January 1946 using an Auster. Scheduled services followed in 1948, principally between Cardiff and the Channel Islands, using a fleet of De Havilland Rapides, and were extended to Paris (via Southampton) in 1953. Services from Bristol were also opened that year and the Rapide bi-planes were joined by a fleet of DH Doves. The Doves were subsequently replaced by Herons and Douglas DC-3s, the latter being introduced from 1954.

In 1958 British European Airways acquired a third share in Cambrian Airways but severe financial problems almost wiped the airline out in 1958/59. It was only the low cost lease/purchase of BEA Pionairs that allowed Cambrian to climb back into the air in 1959. Between 1959 and 1963 Cambrian steadily built up its network of services from Cardiff and Bristol, to the Channel Islands and Paris in particular.

A major expansion occured in 1963 when Cambrian took over BEA's Isle of Man routes, purchasing five ex-BEA Viscount 700s to fly these. Cambrian eventually standardised its fleet on the Viscount with Pionair operations coming to an end on October 31st 1968. The Viscount 700s were gradually replaced by Series-800 aircraft, although two of the earlier models did remain in service until 1977 - operating a feeder link to Prestwick from Belfast and Aberdeen to connect with BA's transatlantic flights.

Cambrian Airways became a wholly owned subsidiary of British European Airways in 1967 and was managed through the holding company - British Air Services. The airline entered the jet age in 1969 with the delivery of the first of four BAC 1-11-400s. These were used on some scheduled services, ie: Cardiff-Bristol-Southampton-Paris, but chiefly operated inclusive tour flights. In October 1973 Cambrian lost its identity and its fleet of BAC 1-11s and Viscounts were repainted to wear the full red, white and blue colouring of British Airways, with small Cambrian titling displayed on the lower forward fuselage. Cambrian officially ceased to exist in 1976.

60

Luton-based Autair began trading as Court Line on January 1st 1970 using a fleet of seven BAC 1-11-400/500s on a wide range of IT charters to holiday resorts throughout the Mediterranean region. By the summer of 1972 inclusive tour charters were being flown from Luton, Birmingham, Bristol, Cardiff, London-Gatwick and Manchester, and the earlier 1-11-400s had been rolled over in favour of a twelve-strong 1-11-500 fleet. The tour companies which used Court Line were principally Clarksons, Wallace Arnold, Pontinental and Hourmont Travel, although many others also used the airline.

When Autair became Court Line it was decided to completely change the airline's image to reflect that of a colourful holiday airline. This may well have been taken to the extreme by the designers which used combinations of turquoise, pink, orange and lilac to colour the fleet, ensuring that no part of the fuselage or fin was left unpainted. The liveries were complimented by silver 'Court' titles and a similarly coloured tail motif. The concept was also adopted by all members of the Court Line Group, including Court Helicopters and LIAT of Antigua.

The Court Line Group also had many other interests and in 1971 purchased a 75% holding in Leeward Islands Air Transport. The Group had already invested in hotels in the region and was rapidly expanding its operations in the Caribbean to attract more British and American tourists. This was one of the reasons behind Court Line ordering two Lockheed TriStars in August 1972, so that winter sun holidays to the Caribbean could be added to its usual range of Mediterranean destinations. Some BAC 1-11s were also transferred to LIAT during the off-peak winter months to ensure maximum utilisation of the fleet.

Named 'Halcyon Days' and 'Halcyon Breeze', the TriStars entered service during the summer of 1973 on inclusive tour services from Luton. Prior to the delivery of these aircraft Court Line had purchased a former Royal Air Force Beverley to transport spare engines to any stranded members of its fleet. This ungainly aircraft arrived at Luton wearing basic Royal Air Force markings, but sadly never entered service with the airline. The 1-11 fleet was occasionally supplemented by leased aircraft but generally remained twelve strong. The airline never took the trouble to repaint any of these leased 1-11s owing to the high costs involved. Altogether, four 1-11s adopted the turquoise theme, three the pink, four the orange and three the lilac. Only one aircraft ever carried two variations of the livery, namely 1-11-500 G-AXMK, which adopted both turquoise and orange themes during its time with the airline.

On August 15th 1974 the airline declared itself bankrupt and ceased trading. Finances had been difficult since April 1973 when Court line came to the rescue of the tour operator Clarksons, which at the time was on the verge of bankruptcy. In January 1974 Court line also acquired Horizon Holidays, but the rising cost of fuel, the poor economic situation and heavy loan repayments finally caught up with the airline, much to the frustration of thousands of holidaymakers either stranded abroad or in possession of worthless tickets. The final Court line movement was the arrival of TriStar G-BAAB at Luton Airport on August 16th at 09.39 hours.

DAN AIR

Dan Air Services Ltd. was founded on May 21st 1953 as a subsidiary of Davies & Newman Ltd., the London Shipping Brokers, from whom its name was derived. The airline initially operated a single Douglas DC-3 on passenger and freight charters from Southend, but as this work built up so the fleet was expanded and in 1956 Dan Air established a new base at Blackbushe. Several Airspeed Ambassadors were acquired in 1959, primarily for its inclusive tour services, although by then the company was also flying some scheduled passenger routes such as Blackbushe to Jersey. Dan Air's operations were gradually transferred to Gatwick Airport prior to the closure of Blackbushe to commercial traffic at midnight on May 31st 1960.

In addition to its scheduled and inclusive tour services Dan Air also made a name for itself hauling freight. This activity utilised Douglas DC-3s, Avro Yorks and Bristol Freighters in the 1950s and early '60s. The Bristol 170s operated the longest route of all, from Blackbushe to Woomera in Australia. This was flown for the British Government to carry rocket parts to the testing range at Woomera, with the Freighter usually taking a month to complete the round trip! Dan Air also operated many BEA freight schedules during the late 1950s and early '60s. A Douglas DC-7 freighter was used from 1966 but as the demand for this work slowly diminished Dan Air decided to concentrate on its passenger operations, retiring its remaining DC-3s and Bristol Freighters by 1970.

Transatlantic charters to the United States were introduced on April 1st 1971 following the introduction of an ex-Pan Am Boeing 707-320 earlier that year. A second 707 was acquired and during 1972 and '73 these aircraft flew numerous passenger charters from Gatwick, Manchester and Prestwick to destinations in the United States and Canada. The '707s were also used on inclusive tour flights from Gatwick, Glasgow and Manchester to the Mediterranean at the height of the holiday season. The acquisition of Skyways International in April 1973 enabled Dan Air to build up a new network of scheduled inter-city services, as well as a large fleet of HS-748s.

Inclusive tour operations proceeded into the jet age in 1966 when Dan Air introduced the first of many Comet 4 aircraft. The type was to remain at the centre of Dan Air's IT operations until 1980, although by this time the airline was also using BAC 1-11s and Boeing 727s. Altogether, the airline operated a total of thirteen Comet 4s, eleven Comet 4Bs and ten Comet 4Cs, and also acquired many others for spares. The original Comet 4s were phased out by May 1974 and replaced by ex-Channel Airways and BEA Airtours Comet 4Bs. The Comet 4C fleet continued to grow until September 1975 when the airline completed the purchase of five aircraft from the Royal Air Force. Dan Air later acquired three Comet 4Cs from Egyptair, but these were ferried to its engineering base at Lasham (in October 1976) to be broken up for spares.

BAC 1-11s were originally introduced from March 1969 and by the summer of 1975 no less than twelve were in operation. The type has served longer than any other in Dan Air service and was instrumental in developing the company's scheduled network in later years. Dan Air's relationship with the Boeing 727 began with the purchase of three series-100 aircraft from Japan Air Lines at the start of the 1973 summer season. The type entered service on April 13th 1973 and following the retirement of the Comets several years later it was become the mainstay of Dan Air's IT operations, with the fleet later expanded to include 727-200s as well.

Many liveries have been associated with Dan Air over the years, although by and large the airline tended to revise existing designs at regular intervals instead of changing its image completely. The featured liveries illustrate some of the changes that took place from the mid-'sixties as Dan Air progressively worked towards its final blue and red design. The black and red livery adopted by the Ambassadors and Yorks is sadly missing from this selection, but does appear as a secondary feature on page 42 where Ambassador G-AMAE is seen parked behind a Trident of BKS.

The livery illustrated by Douglas DC-7 G-ATAB welcomed the first Comets to the fleet in 1966 at a time when various designs and colour combinations were in use, the most notable deviation from the usual red and black colouring being that of two leased DC-4 aircraft, which upheld their existing green liveries. A variation of the Comet scheme was adopted by the first BAC 1-11-400 aircraft introduced in March/April 1969, although this revision (illustrated by G-AZED) remained synonymous to that particular family of aircraft.

The next major livery change occured in January 1971 when Dan Air received its first Boeing 707, registered G-AYSL, which introduced the red tail colouring illustrated by sistership G-AZTG. With the earlier piston-engined aircraft having left the fleet by now, it became the first Dan Air livery to be adopted by all types operated, including Comet, 1-11, Boeing 707, 727-100 (from March 1973), HS-748 and also Viscount aircraft. All aircraft, with the exception of the Boeing 707s, later adopted a modified version of this scheme (illustrated by Comet 4C G-BDIT), which effectively brought this classic era to an end. By 1980 the airline had introduced new red and blue colouring and the red and black combination that had been associated with Dan Air for so long faded with the last Comet aircraft. The new image was adopted by the Boeing 727-100 (and 727-200 aircraft introduced from March 1980), the HS-748s and 1-11s, and in later years also adorned modern Airbus A300, British Aerospace 146 and Boeing 737 airliners as Dan Air embarked on a major fleet modernisation programme.

CP AIR (CANADIAN PACIFIC AIRLINES)

CP Air was formed as Canadian Pacific Airlines Ltd. on January 30th 1942 by the Canadian Pacific Railway to take over and unify a group of ten small Canadian bush operators, the most important of these being Canadian Airways. Initially, the company operated networks in west and north-west Canada, in the Winnipeg area and in Quebec, as part of an overall railway/ship/air CPR system. Canadian Pacific expanded overseas in July 1949 when a scheduled route was inaugurated to Sydney, via Hawaii, Fiji and Auckland, using a fleet of four Canadair C-4 Argonauts. Another trans-Pacific service later reached Tokyo and Hong Kong, via the Aleutians. In 1953 the airline opened services to Mexico City and Lima (subsequently extended to Santiago and Buenos Aires), by which time a fleet of Douglas DC-6s had been incorporated. This was followed in 1955 by a trans-Polar route between Vancouver and Amsterdam, and then in 1957 by a transatlantic service to Madrid and Lisbon. Between 1958 and 1959 the airline took delivery of eight turboprop Bristol Britannias to replace DC-6Bs on the long haul routes across the Pacific, and to Europe. The turboprop Britannias were also used to expand the existing network, opening scheduled trans-continental services in May 1960 and also a new route to Rome. Jet operations commenced during the summer of 1961 following the delivery of three Rolls-Royce Conway-powered Douglas DC-8s and the relatively new Britannias were soon relegated to secondary routes and charter work. The fleet was later standardised on DC-8-40 and DC-8-63 aircraft, the latter introduced from January 1968.

With the introduction of the DC-8-63s at the beginning of 1968 Canadian Pacific Airlines became known as CP Air and adopted the livery illustrated by Boeing 747-200B C-FCRD 'Empress of Australia' (one of four operated by the airline from November 1973). This colourful design was also applied to 727-100s (from April 1970), 727-200s (from March 1975), 737-200s (from October 1968) and McDonnell Douglas DC-10-30s (from March 1979). CP Air later joined forces with Pacific Western Airlines to form Canadian Airlines International on April 26th 1987.

CSA CZECHOSLOVAK AIRLINES

CSA was founded on July 19th 1923 as Ceskoslovenske Statni Aerolinie and began operations on October 28th between Prague and Bratislava using ex-military A-14 bi-planes (licence-built Hansa-Bradenburgs). International services, inaugurated on July 1st 1930, were rapidly expanded throughout the European continent but, on March 15th 1939, CSA had to suspend all activities following the partitioning of the country on the eve of the second World War. The present company was formed on September 15th 1945 when the operations of the pre-war CSA, CLS (Ceskoslovenska Letecka Spolecnost) - which had provided international services since 1927, and the war-time SLAS (Slovenska Letecka Akciova Spolecnost) were concentrated into a single unit. The makeshift fleet of the immediate post war period was later standardised on Soviet supplied Ilyushin Il-12Bs and Lisunov Li-2s from 1949, of which ten and eight respectively were in service by 1953. The transition to jet aircraft was made as early as 1957 when CSA took delivery of the first of three ordered Tupolev Tu-104As. The airline eventually operated six of these aircraft, together with three Tu-124Vs delivered from November 1964. Between 1957 and 1958 CSA also received twenty-five locally produced Avia/Ilyushin Il-14s to replace the earlier Li-2s and Il-12Bs, and from January 1960 turboprop Ilyushin Il-18s began to supplement the Tupolev jets and open new routes beyond the range of these aircraft.

The livery illustrated by Il-18V OK-OAC was introduced by the Tu-104As from November 1957 and remained the standard colouring until the arrival of the first Il-62s exactly ten years later. The new OK-jet style introduced by the new Ilyushin jet was not adopted by any of the Il-14s (phased-out by 1977), Tu-104As (phased-out by 1974) or Tu-124Vs (phased out by 1972), but in later years two Il-18s were repainted to wear similar markings. The older Tupolev jets were gradually replaced by Tu-134s (from December 1971) and the piston-engined Il-14s by Yakovlev Yak-40s (from October 1974).

DELTA AIR TRANSPORT

Antwerp-based Delta Air Transport was formed in 1967 to serve the region with air-taxi and general charter services, and commenced operations using a fleet of light aircraft and Douglas DC-3s. The airline found plenty of work for its aircraft and expanded its activities to a large degree during the years that followed. Scheduled passenger services were opened between Antwerp and Amsterdam on behalf of KLM, which acquired a 33.3% holding in the airline, while the volume of charter work soon outgrew the original DC-3 fleet.

Major expansion, starting with the introduction of an ex-BIAS Douglas DC-6 in December 1971, was evident throughout the following twelve months. During the summer of 1972 the airline acquired four Convair 440s from Iberia and increased its Douglas DC-6 fleet to three, following the purchase of aircraft from Kar Air and Icelandair. The DC-6 fleet was expanded again that winter and by January of the following year Delta Air Transport was operating five of these aircraft. Over the next two to three years the fleet composition was changed to include another two Convair 440s and fewer DC-6s. Another major transformation took place in 1977 when the airline replaced its four remaining Cv-440s with four Fairchild-Hiller FH-227Bs acquired from Ozark Airlines, while the company's association with the DC-6 was to end with the sale of OO-VFG in March 1978.

The livery illustrated by Convair 440 OO-UVG was eventually toned down to feature white cabin roof and fin colouring and red (later blue) cheatlines and tail markings.

EAST AFRICAN AIRWAYS CORPORATION

East African Airways was incorporated on January 1st 1946 as the national airline of the four countries which comprised British East Africa, namely Kenya (67.7% shareholding), Uganda (22.6%), Tanganyika (9.0% and Zanzibar (0.7%). Operations began with six de Havilland Rapides on April 3rd 1946, linking Nairobi with Mombasa, Tanga, Zanzibar and Dar-es-Salaam. The first international service was inaugurated in 1949 to Durban,.followed in the late 1950's with further extensions to London, Khartoum, Aden, Karachi and Bombay.

The livery illustrated by Douglas DC-3 5X-AAQ, an aircraft originally acquired by EAAC as VP-KJR in February 1952, was introduced with the delivery of the airline's first Comet 4s in the summer of 1960. The cheatline colours were extracted from the flags of the participating nations, while the tail motif ingeniously featured the flags of Kenya, Uganda and Tanzania (formerly Tanganyika and Zanzibar). All aircraft delivered from then on, including Fokker F.27-200s from October 1962, BAC Super VC-10s from October 1966, Twin Otters from July 1967 and Douglas DC-9-32s from December 1970, adopted this scheme. The earlier Douglas DC-3s were also repainted although three Canadair C-4 Argonauts, operated from the summer of 1957, remained in basic BOAC markings. A Boeing 707 was also operated in this livery by subsidiary Simbair, which had been formed in May 1971 to undertake cargo charters.

When East African Airways ceased operations on January 22nd 1977 its international network reached London, Paris, Athens, Copenhagen, Frankfurt, Rome, Zurich, Bombay and Karachi. In addition, the airline also served numerous points within Africa.

EASTERN AIR LINES

Eastern Air Lines can trace its history back to May 1st 1928 when Pitcairn Aviation (established in April 1926) opened a mail service between New York and Atlanta, using a fleet of single-engined 'Mailwing' aircraft, designed and built by Harold F. Pitcairn. On July 10th 1949 the company was acquired by North American Aviation and changed its name to Eastern Air Transport Inc. on January 17th 1930, later to be known as Eastern Air Lines from March 29th 1938 following extensive re-organisation. A number of small companies were absorbed during these early years, including New York Airways and Ludington Airlines. On June 1st 1956, Eastern extended its network to Ottawa and Montreal in Canada, and to Bermuda following the purchase of Colonial Airlines. Other more recent takeovers included those of Mackey Airlines (January 1967) and Caribbean Atlantic Airlines-Caribair (in May 1973). The latter had been formed in February 1939 and operated Douglas DC-9-30s and Convair 640s on services from San Juan (Puerto Rico) to points throughout the Caribbean islands and to Miami.

The airline was instrumental in establishing low fare, no reservation shuttle services, which it originally inaugurated between New York, Boston and Washington on April 30th 1961. Its commitment to simplifying air travel within the New York-Boston-Washington triangle made news again in 1968 when Eastern evaluated the use of high-capacity STOL aircraft on these well-travelled routes. Working closely with McDonnell Douglas, Eastern used a pre-production Breguet 941 built to French Air Force specification (illustrated) between August 23rd and November 5th of that year in an effort to see how STOL traffic could be segregated out from regular airway and terminal area users. A similar experiment was later undertaken by American Airlines from Chicago but plans to develop and build the French aircraft under licence as the McDonnell Douglas 188 (or the advanced model 210G) came to nothing. Eastern's pioneering work with this STOL development was not unusual, seeing as the airline had been first in the world to place many new and commercially unproven airliners into service. These included the first true civil model of the Lockheed Constellation, the 'gold plate' L-649 (in May 1947), the original L-1049 Super Constellation (on December 17th 1951), the Lockheed L.188A Electra (on January 12th 1959), the Boeing 727-100 (on February 1st 1964), the Lockheed TriStar (on April 15th 1972) and finally the Boeing 757-200 (on January 1st 1983).

Jet operations were initiated in January 1960 using the first of sixteen ordered Douglas DC-8-21s, later joined by fifteen leased Boeing 720s from August 1961. By early 1965 Eastern's fleet consisted of fifteen DC-8-21s, fifteen Boeing 720s (ten leased), forty-three Douglas DC-7Bs, twenty-five Boeing 727-100s (five leased), thirty-nine Lockheed L.188A Electras, ten L-1049Gs, 10 L-1049Cs (N6225C illustrating in original markings), twelve L.1049s and twenty Convair 440s, while fifteen 727-100s and twenty-four Douglas DC-9-10s were on order. The older propliners were phased-out by the end of the decade and replaced by an assortment of 727s, DC-9s and DC-8-61/63PFs, while the Electras soldiered on a little longer. Although an order for four Boeing 747-100s was cancelled, Eastern did briefly operate the type on services from New York to Miami and San Juan from January 1971 (using aircraft leased from Pan Am), prior to the introduction of TriStars from April of the following year.

Eastern eventually ceased operations on January 18th 1991 following an earlier Chapter 11 filing, by which time its fleet consisted mostly of 727-200s, 757s, DC-9-30/50s, TriStars and Airbus A300B4s.

EURAVIA

Euravia was set up by Universal Sky Tours, one of Britain's leading inclusive-tour holiday companies, and commenced operations on May 5th 1962 with a fleet of three ex-El Al Lockheed L-049 Constellations. The name Euravia was chosen due to the fact that Britain had applied to join the EEC in 1962 and closer links with Europe were anticipated. While Luton became the main base of operations, a secondary station was established at Manchester Airport to cater for Universal Sky Tours' interests in the north of the country. The summer of 1962 proved to be a busy one for the new airline, with numerous flights being made chiefly from Luton or Manchester to Palma and Perpignan. So hectic was the level of demand that the airline's management decided additional capacity was needed. That materialised in September 1962 when Euravia took over the British airline, Skyways. Skyways operated a fleet of five Constellations in addition to Avro Yorks, and Euravia quickly merged these into its own fleet to give eight operational Constellations for the 1963 summer season (G-AHEL illustrated). For the summer of 1963 flights were again operated from Luton and Manchester, but other U.K. departure points were added in the form of Liverpool and Newcastle. The Constellations also maintained the Skyways scheduled services to Tunis, Malta and Cyprus, although these were discontinued by April 1964. The summer of 1964 brought further route expansion with new U.K. departure points including Birmingham, Blackpool and Cardiff. The number of European holiday destinations was also widening to include not just airfields in Spain and France, but also some destinations in Austria and Yugoslavia. The more distant Canary Islands were also added to the network, the Constellations taking about eight hours to complete the trip from England to the Canaries. By now the time had come to find a replacement for these ageing aircraft and subsequently the Bristol Britannia was chosen for this task. On August 16th 1964 the airline's name was changed to Britannia Airways and a fleet of ex-BOAC Britannia 102s eventually replaced the Constellations.

EUROPE AERO SERVICE

Europe Aero Service was formed in July 1965 as a subsidiary of Societe Aero-Sahara and began scheduled operations a year later with a service from Perpignan to Palma using a small fleet of Vickers Vikings. The airline later acquired two ex-Globe Air Handley Page Heralds in the summer of 1968 and a new Nord 262 in November 1969. These were used on scheduled services between Nimes and Lyon and on short haul routes to Geneva, Ajaccio, Bastia and Valencia.

In September 1971 Europe Aero Service purchased the assets of Trans Union, including a fleet of three Douglas DC-6s, and subsequently began to break new ground in the charter field. By this time the earlier Viking and Nord 262 aircraft had been sold. Major expansion followed in 1972 when EAS completed the purchase of five Vickers Vanguard 952s from Air Canada, including one configured for cargo operations. The two remaining Douglas DC-6s were sold during the summer of 1973 as additional Vanguards were acquired. Altogether, EAS purchased a total of sixteen Vanguards between 1972 and 1976, of which thirteen entered service in either passenger or freight modes. The Vanguards were eventually phased out at the turn of the 'eighties as EAS focused on jet operations using Caravelle and Boeing 727 equipment.

The livery illustrated by Vanguard 952 F-BVRZ was technically a hybrid scheme based on the fuselage and fin colouring of Air Canada. To compliment this the Heralds were repainted to wear a similar shade of red but to the outline of the original pale blue livery. In later years a new livery, based on white fuselage and fin colouring with diagonal red stripes, was adopted by all members of the fleet.

EGYPTAIR (UNITED ARAB AIRLINES)

Egyptair can trace its history back to June 7th 1932 when the British company Airwork Ltd. entered into an agreement with the Misr Bank of Cairo to form Misr Airwork. With technical and operational assistance from Airwork the airline commenced operations in July 1933, initially between Cairo and Mersa Matruh (via Alexandria), using a modest fleet of de Havilland DH.84 Dragons. International services were inaugurated in 1934 with connections to Lydda and Haifa. In the years following the war the airline re-equipped with Vickers Vikings and Sud Est SE.161 Languedocs. Airwork withdrew its interest in 1949 and the airline became known simply as Misrair (Egyptair). The Vikings were later supplemented by Viscount 700s, introduced from early 1956, as the airline continued to spread its network further afield. Misrair introduced two Comet 4Cs to its international network during the summer of 1960, although by the arrival of a third aircraft later that year its name had been changed to United Arab Airlines.

Following the formation of the short-lived United Arab Republic in 1960 the airline formed a partnership with Syrian Airlines, which took effect from January 1st 1961. Three ex-SAS Douglas DC-6Bs that had been acquired by UAA in early 1961 were transferred to the newly created Syrian Arab Airlines in October that year, although the airline later renewed its interest in the type by purchasing a total of seven DC-6Bs from Pan American and Northwest from March 1964. A further six Comet 4Cs were delivered between June 1961 and December 1966 and the remaining Vikings and Viscounts were phased out. Domestic services continued to be operated in the name of Misrair and a fleet of ten Antonov An-24s was incorporated in 1965/66 to meet the requirements of this subsidiary.

For many years United Arab Airlines sampled the products of both western and Soviet manufacturers and seemed helplessly unable to choose between the two. In September 1968 the airline took delivery of a new Boeing 707, and only weeks later introduced the first of four Ilyushin Il-18Ds (SU-AOY illustrated). A further three 707s were added between 1969 and 1970 and then from June 1971 the airline leased Ilyushin Il-62s from Aeroflot, with at least four being operational at any one time. Eventually, the airline decided to order another four Boeing 707s to replace the leased Il-62s from the summer of 1973. A final flirtation with Soviet aircraft occured in December of that year when Egyptair, as UAA had now become, received the first of eight ordered Tupolev Tu-154s. These were later returned to the Soviet Union, together with the two remaining Il-18Ds, as Egyptair turned to the Boeing 737 for its domestic and regional requirements. As for the ten Antonov An-24s introduced by Misrair during the mid-sixties, all but three had been written-off by 1970 and those that survived were later placed into store at Cairo.

The name Egyptair was adopted on October 10th 1971 for both domestic and international operations and a new livery, featuring the head of Horus, was introduced to replace the former United Arab identity. However, it took many years for this new image to filter through and during this period many different livery combinations were used. One example is illustrated by Il-62 SU-AWJ, which is seen wearing joint Aeroflot/UAA markings but with Aeroflot titles.

Flying Tigers was initially incorporated on June 25th 1945 as National Skyway Freight Corporation, having been formed by twelve members of a famed group of World War II combat pilots, known as the 'Flying Tigers'. Operations commenced from a two car garage on a California airport, initially using a fleet of fourteen Budd Conestoga freighters which had been specially built for the U.S. Navy, later joined by ex-military Douglas C-54s. The Flying Tigers name was adopted in early 1946 and the company soon replaced the ungainly Conestoga's with war surplus Douglas C-47s. In the months following World War II a great demand arose for overseas airlift. With Government aircraft usage at a premium, Flying Tigers became a prime U.S. air carrier and soon claimed the largest airlift ever performed by a single contractor - the supply of General MacArthur's occupational forces in Japan. In subsequent years, the airline continued to play key roles in the military contract field, flying up to a third of the U.S. Government's Military Airlift Command charter flights.

Coast to Coast cargo services were inaugurated in 1949 and eventually served destinations such as New York, Boston, Syracuse, Hartford/Springfield, Birmingham, Buffalo, Philadelphia, Cleveland, Detroit, Chicago, Milwaukee, Los Angeles, San Francisco/Oakland, Portland and Seattle on a scheduled basis. In 1969 Flying Tigers was awarded a route across the Pacific to Tokyo, Okinawa, Seoul, Taipei, Hong Kong and Manilla, which was officially inaugurated in September of that year, while services to Europe followed in October 1980 following the company's acquisition of Seaboard World Airlines

In 1949 Flying Tigers purchased twenty-three Curtiss C-46 Commandos, acquired the largest fleet of Douglas DC-6A freighters ever placed into operation in 1953 and inaugurated its fleet of fifteen Lockheed L-1049H Super Constellations in 1957. In 1961 the airline purchased its first turbine powered freighters, the Canadair CL-44 Swingtails, of which ten were in service by April 1962. Jet operations were started in October 1965 following the delivery of two Boeing 707-320Cs, which were supplemented by several leased aircraft until the type was phased out by Flying Tigers in 1969. A fleet of Douglas DC-8-63Fs was incorporated from 1968 and in August 1974 the airline added the first of many Boeing 747 freighters.

The original Douglas C-47s, used from 1946, displayed shark-like teeth on the forward underside and intricate Flying Tiger Line titling across the cabin roof. This concept was evident in a subsequent livery, using an outline of the C-47s cockpit section, complete with teeth, in a motif displayed as a continuation of the forward cheatline arrangement - as illustrated by Curtiss C-46 N392N. This scheme was also worn by the DC-6s and Super Constellations, although in its original form the titles were in script as opposed to the solid upper case lettering seen here. The stylised 'T' motif was introduced by the first CL-44s in June 1961 as part of a completely new image, also featuring broken cheatlines (illustrated by N446T). This scheme was later adopted by the Boeing 707s and revised to include a blue coloured fin with the arrival of the first DC-8s in 1968. A similar livery was adopted by the Boeing 747s but with the cheatlines replaced by a blue, white and red fuselage sash.

In 1977 the tail motif was dropped in favour of white 'Flying Tigers' titling, only to be reinstated as part of another livery change ten years later. The born again motif was, however, only given a short lease of life for on August 7th 1989 the company was acquired by Federal Express.

GERMANAIR

Germanair was originally known as Sudwestflug and commenced operations in September 1965 using a single Douglas DC-6, registered D-ABAH. The name Germanair was adopted in October 1968 following the purchase of two DC-6s from Transavia, and the airline soon established itself as a major holiday charter airline, flying German tourists to the sun filled resorts of the Mediterranean. Jet operations started in April 1969, initially with a leased Douglas DC-9-15, and the fleet was later standardised on the BAC 1-11-500. By March 1970 Germanair was using three 1-11-500s while the DC-6 fleet had been disbanded.

Major expansion followed in the summer of 1972 when the airline took delivery of four new Fokker Fellowships and added two ex-Paninternational BAC 1-11-500s. The 1-11 fleet was trimmed two years later as Germanair prepared for the arrival of its first Airbus Industrie A300B4, which entered service in May 1975. The Fellowships were phased out by the start of the following summer to coincide with the delivery of a second Airbus from Toulouse, with three going on lease to Itavia and the other being sold to Aerolineas Argentinas. The last two aircraft returned from Italy in November 1977 and were later sold to TAT of France.

Germanair eventually joined forces with Munich-based Bavaria Flug, which operated a large fleet of BAC 1-11s on inclusive tour charters, to form Germany's third largest airline, and from January 1st 1977 all operations were conducted under the title of Bavaria Germanair. Inclusive tour charters were flown to destinations throughout the Mediterranean, Canary Isles and North Africa, mainly from Munich and Frankfurt. Bavaria-Germanair was merged into Hapag Lloyd two years later, in January 1979, at which time its fleet consisted of four Airbus A300B4s and seven BAC 1-11-500s.

The red and black colouring of the Douglas DC-6s was also adopted by the original BAC 1-11-500 fleet (D-AMUR illustrated), introduced from October 1969. A new red and blue livery was evaluated by Germanair from May 1971 but the airline eventually selected the design illustrated by Airbus Industrie A300B4 D-AMAX, which welcomed the first Fokker Fellowships to the fleet from March 1972. The red and blue colouring remained in use following the merger with Bavaria Flug as part of a joint Bavaria-Germanair image.

Germanair

GARUDA INDONESIAN AIRWAYS

Garuda was created on March 31st 1950 by the Government of the newly-independent State of Indonesia and KLM, to succeed the pre-war KNILM (established on October 15th 1928), and the post-war Inter-Island Division of the Dutch carrier. KLM initially provided technical and management assistance and the new airline commenced operations later that year with the fleet left by KNILM, which included Douglas DC-3s and Catalinas. These were soon supplemented by eight Convair 240s and, following nationalisation in March 1954, by several Convair 340s. International routes to Bangkok, Manila, Hong Kong and Tokyo were opened during the summer of 1961 following the delivery of three new Lockheed L.188C Electras, while jet operations were inaugurated three years later when, in September 1963, Garuda received the first of three ordered Convair 990As. During March 1965 a new service was opened to Peking (via Canton and Phnom-Penh) and a route to Europe, via Bangkok/Phnom-Penh, Bombay, Cairo, Prague, Paris and Amsterdam, followed using Douglas DC-8 equipment (initially leased from KLM). A fleet of three Douglas DC-8-50s eventually replaced the Convair 990As on all international services while Fokker F.27-600s, Douglas DC-9-30s and later F.28 Fellowships began to modernise the airline's domestic and regional operation from 1969 onwards. The expansion of Garuda's international network led to the acquisition of wide-bodied McDonnell Douglas DC-10-30 and Boeing 747 aircraft in later years, with Airbus A300B4s increasing capacity on regional routes from January 1982.

The name Garuda originated from a large, legendary bird of Indonesian folklore, which became a key feature of the airline's livery for many years. The colourscheme illustrated by Convair 990A PK-GJC took Garuda into the jet age and superseded a similar design that had been adopted by the Convair and Electra aircraft, again based on the national colours of red and white. In later years a new 'garuda' motif was displayed on the fin, although with the introduction of the present livery in September 1985 the bird was reinstated.

GHANA AIRWAYS

Ghana Airways was formed on July 4th 1958 by the Ghanian Government (60%) and BOAC (40%) to take over the operations of West African Airways Corporation in the former British colony known as the Gold Coast. BOAC provided a Boeing Stratocruiser which, on July 16th, inaugurated the new airline's first service between Accra and London. The airline became fully operational on October 1st 1958 when it assumed the domestic and regional operations of WAAC.

Following the purchase of BOAC's shareholding, Ghana Airways became entirely state-owned on February 14th 1961. Between 1960 and 1965 the airline operated a mixed fleet which included eight Ilyushin Il-18Vs, one Antonov An-12, two Bristol Britannias, four Douglas DC-3s, and three Viscount 800s (delivered new in October/November 1961). The Il-18s operated the main African trunk routes, including Accra-Kano-Khartoum-Addis Ababa and Accra-Ouagadougou-Bamako-Rabat, as well as an Accra-Kano-Cairo-Beirut connection and services to Moscow and London. By June 1965 the airline had taken delivery of two Vickers VC-10s which replaced turboprop aircraft on all mainline international routes and operated services to London both non-stop and via Rome. An order for a third VC-10 was cancelled while the existing fleet was reduced to just one aircraft from June 1965. The DC-3s and Viscounts were later replaced by Hawker Siddeley 748s and Fokker Fellowships respectively, and a McDonnell Douglas DC-9-50 was added in July 1978 to supplement these aircraft.

The livery illustrated by VC-10 9G-ABO remained the standard colouring of Ghana Airways until the introduction of Fokker F.28s from May 1974, when the present design was adopted. However, the flagship VC-10 was operated in a combination of old and new markings for more than a year and was not fully repainted until the spring of 1976.

IBERIA

Iberia emerged on July 7th 1940 from a long line of predecessor companies dating back to 1921, and was given exclusive rights to operate services within Spain, the Spanish Territories and internationally. Initial shareholding was split between between the Government (51%), and Deutsche Luft Hansa and other interests (49%), but all shares were purchased by Instituto Nacional de Industria (INI), a Government concern, on September 30th 1944. In June 1941 services were established within Spain and to Palma, the Canaries, Morocco and the Spanish territories in North Africa, but most of these were suspended less than a year later owing to difficulties in obtaining fuel and did not gain any real momentum until after the war.

In 1944, Iberia adopted a fleet of Douglas DC-3s which had been abandoned in Spain by the USAAF, while further examples were purchased from ex-US military stocks between 1946 and 1949. These aircraft, together with new and used Douglas DC-4s delivered from the summer of 1946, were instrumental in developing the airline's scheduled international network. Services were soon opened to London and Rome while the longer range Douglas DC-4s concentrated on building a network to Latin America. The introduction of three Lockheed L-1049E Super Constellations in June and July 1954 coincided with the inauguration of regular services to New York. The fleet was later expanded with the delivery of two new L-1049Gs during the summer of 1957 (EC-AMP illustrated) and four used aircraft (leased or purchased) from March 1961. Between 1957 and 1963 the airline also added sixteen Convair 440s to supplement and eventually replace the Douglas DC-3s on short to medium haul international services.

Jet operations were initiated following the delivery of three Douglas DC-8-50s during the summer of 1961, which began to replace the long-haul Constellations. On November 21st 1960 the airline signed a contract to purchase four Caravelle 6Rs for delivery between February and April 1962. These aircraft effectively replaced the Douglas DC-4s, while the nine remaining Super Constellations were converted to freighters from 1963 as the Caravelle and DC-8 fleets were expanded. Iberia went on to acquire a total of twenty Caravelles (thirteen '6Rs and seven '10Rs), signing its final order with the manufacturer on November 4th 1966. Another eight DC-8-50s (including one all-cargo model) were delivered from October 1962, and between August 1968 and December 1970 the airline also added six Super DC-8-63s.

An offer to buy the Caravelle 12 was rejected by Iberia and the airline subsequently turned its attention towards the Douglas DC-9-30, initially ordering twelve aircraft for delivery from June 1967. A fleet of Fokker Friendships was acquired to replace the Convair 440s in domestic use while three Fellowships were added in 1970 to facilitate pilot conversions to jet aircraft, during the course of operating normal passenger and cargo services for the airline. Sixteen Boeing 727-200s were ordered for fleet introduction between April 1972 and May 1973, at which point the remaining Caravelles were transferred to Aviaco. Douglas DC-8s continued to supplement the '727s on European routes until they too were replaced, by DC-10-30s and Boeing 747s on trans continental routes and by Airbus A300B4 on the high density European routes, the latter from February 1981.

The livery illustrated by Caravelle 6R EC-AVZ was introduced prior to the arrival of the first DC-8-63s during the summer of 1968, the initial DC-9s having adopted the previous scheme with Iberia titles repeated on the fin. This concept was actually continued by the DC-8-63s, as the long, narrow body of these aircraft could comfortably accommodate titles at both ends of the cabin roof.

IRAQI AIRWAYS

Iraqi Airways was founded in December 1945 as a subsidiary of the Government-owned Iraqi State Railways and inaugurated its first service on January 29th 1946 between Baghdad and the main port of Basra - using de Havilland Rapides. International services followed on June 14th 1946 and were extended to Europe less than two years later when, on May 1st 1946, Vickers Viking YI-ABQ left Baghdad to mark the opening of a new monthly service to London, the journey taking three days to complete. The Vikings were replaced by a fleet of Viscount 700s from October 1955, which established regular connections linking Baghdad with Bahrain, Kuwait, Dhahran, Basra, Mosul, Beirut, Damascus, Teheran, Cairo, Vienna, Istanbul, Prague, Rome, Paris, Frankfurt and London. Jet operations were inaugurated following the delivery of three Trident 1Es between October 1965 and May 1966 while the Viscounts were relegated to domestic use, later to be replaced by Antonov An-24s. With the introduction of the Tridents new services were introduced to Karachi, Delhi, East Berlin and Copenhagen, while some of the existing routes were extended to include stops at Athens, Vienna and Geneva.

Boeing 707 operations began in May 1974 using two aircraft leased from Donaldson International, and with this type Iraqi Airways changed the livery that had been in use since the Viking era. However, in its original form the design was based on the existing colouring of Donaldson (illustrated) and it was not until the delivery of the airline's first 707-320C and 737-200C aircraft in August of that year that the full extent of this change became known. The new livery was later applied to Boeing 727-200 and 747-200C aircraft (introduced from March and June 1976 respectively), and by a fleet of Ilyushin Il-76s operated for the Government from 1978 - replacing earlier Antonov An-12s.

ITAVIA (AEROLINEE ITAVIA)

Aerolinee Itavia commenced operations from Urbe Airport (Rome) in July 1959 using an eight-seat De Havilland Dove, having been founded in April of the previous year. A regular route between Rome, Genoa and Sienna was opened in the Spring of 1960 as the company began a new relationship with the larger DH.114 Heron, purchasing an ex-Silver City Airways aircraft and later six from Nigeria Airways. Aerolinee Itavia was forced to suspend operations in October 1960 following a fatal crash and did not resume flying until May 1962, by which time the Herons had been replaced by a small fleet of Douglas DC-3s and a new base had been established at Ciampino Airport. The DC-3s were soon replaced by a modern fleet of Handley Page Heralds, and following a somewhat tough baptism the airline finally settled down to concentrate on developing a scheduled domestic network.

The company took delivery of three new Fokker Fellowships during the winter of 1969/70 and added another two from LTU in April 1973 to replace the Heralds. Itavia also built up a fleet of Douglas DC-9-10s from October 1971. Additional F-28s and DC-9s were leased-in during the years that followed, including DC-9-51 equipment, as Itavia sought to expand its scheduled and charter activities.

The airline's safety record was far from enviable, with accidents claiming examples of all types operated from 1960. It was therefore not surprising that when DC-9-15 I-TIGI crashed into the Tyrrhenian Sea on June 27th 1980 Itavia's operating licence was revoked and the airline forced to shut down. At the time of its demise Itavia was Italy's second largest domestic airline.

KAR AIR

Kar Air was formed in 1947 as a subsidiary of Veljekset Karhumaki, an old established aircraft manufacturing, overhaul and maintenance organisation. Operations commenced in June 1950 with a scheduled summer service between Helsinki and Joensuu using a de Havilland Rapide. The company changed its name to Karhumaki Airways in 1951 and expanded its network to include Kuopio, Jyvaskula, Vaasa and Sundsvall (Sweden), by which time a fleet of Lockheed Lodestars had replaced the original Rapide bi-plane.

Charter services were introduced during the winter of 1951 and in April 1952 a route linking Helsinki, Tampere and Vaasa was taken over from Aero O/Y (Finnair) and extended to Stockholm. The Lodestars were later replaced by ex-SAS Douglas DC-3s, although one of these aircraft was converted for geological survey work and remained a permanent fixture of the fleet for many years. Following heavy financial losses, the company was re-organised in December 1956 with capital from the Finnish Steamship Company, at which time the name Kar Air was adopted. Two Convair 440s were added from June 1957 but renewed financial problems led to the acquisition of a 51% holding interest by Aero O/Y in November 1963, which included the take-over of Kar Air's scheduled routes and the Convairs which had been used to operate them.

The company continued to concentrate on charter and inclusive tour work which became largely the responsibility of a fleet of Douglas DC-6 aircraft, the first of which having been introduced in May 1961. Three of these aircraft were in use by February 1965 and remained at the centre of charter and IT operations until the introduction of a Douglas DC-8-50 in 1972, prior to which two of the DC-6s were sold. The third aircraft had undertaken a 'swing tail' conversion in April 1968 and operated charters and scheduled cargo flights under contract to Finnair until the summer of 1982. The tail colouring of this freighter was later changed to feature a cartoon bear pushing a sack barrow (illustrated), the humour reflecting the fact that is was one of the last DC-6s to be operated in Europe.

LUFTHANSA

Lufthansa can trace its history back to January 6th 1926 when two of Germany's leading airlines (Deutcher Aero Lloyd and Junkers Luftverkehr AG) were merged to form Deutsche Luft Hansa. D.L.H. quickly became one of the world's leading airlines and embarked upon many well known pioneering flights which took it far beyond Europe in its quest to establish a worldwide service network. The airline continued its activities during the war until its last flight left Berlin in May 1945.

Lufthansa began post war operations on April 1st 1955, initially using four Convair 340s on services between Hamburg, Dusseldorf, Cologne, Frankfurt and Munich. Madrid and London were soon added to the network and by June the airline was crossing the Atlantic with Lockheed Super Constellations to New York. Major expansion followed as the airline introduced Douglas DC-3s, Vickers Viscount 800s and Lockheed L.1649A Starliners to its growing network, while the original Convair 340s were converted to -440 standard and joined by several others.

The first jet aircraft began to arrive in February 1960 in the form of Rolls Royce Conway-powered Boeing 707-400s, which eventually replaced the relatively new Starliners and Constellations on long-haul routes. Lufthansa went on to become a leading customer of the Boeing Aeroplane Company, taking delivery of 720s (from March 1961), 707-320Bs (February 1963), 727-100/200s (from February 1964/1973 respectively), 707-320Cs (from November 1965), all models of the 737 (from December 1967) and various models of the 747 (from March 1970).

The yellow and blue colouring of Lufthansa has adopted many forms and been associated with a variety of aircraft types over the years, perhaps none more unusual than Curtiss C-46 freighter N9891Z (illustrated) - leased from Capital Airlines in 1964.

KLM Royal Dutch Airlines was formed on October 7th 1919 and commenced operations on May 17th 1920 using a two-seat de Havilland DH.16 between Amsterdam and London (Croydon). From these humble beginnings, KLM's operations spread throughout the European continent and beyond. On October 1st a proving flight was made to Djakarta (Netherlands East Indies), for the purpose of providing a link with the Dutch colonies and the setting up of a local network, which was initiated on November 1st 1928 by an associate company, KNILM. In a similar way, services were established to the colonies in the West Indies, with local operations starting on January 19th 1935. These airlines provided the foundations of the present day carriers known as Garuda and ALM respectively. By 1939 KLM was serving sixty-one destinations in twenty-seven countries, with the majority of these routes flown with Douglas DC-2/DC-3 equipment, the latter introduced from 1936. The airline suffered heavily during the war, when most of its aircraft were destroyed and captured by the Luftwaffe, but managed to continue its West Indian services without interruption.

With the liberation of Holland air services were slowly resumed using Douglas DC-3 and later DC-4 aircraft, and by August 1946 most European capitals were again being served. The rebuilding of KLM's route network and fleet continued over the next few years, equipment purchased during this period including six Lockheed L-049 Constellations (from May 1946), twenty-two L-749/As (from August 1947), eight Douglas DC-6s (from March 1948) and twelve Convair 240s (from August 1948). Many of these original post war airliners were replaced as newer and improved models became available, and in a second phase of expansion and fleet modernisation KLM took delivery of nine Douglas DC-6Bs (from May 1952), two Douglas DC-6As (from July 1953), twenty-two L-1049C/E/ G Super Constellations (from June 1953) and twelve Convair 340s (from September 1953) - subsequently converted to Cv-440 standard. In later years KLM also ordered the Douglas DC-7C, receiving fifteen of these aircraft between April 1957 and December 1958.

Jet operations started following the delivery of the first of eight Douglas DC-8-30s from March 1960, later joined by eight series-50 aircraft delivered between April 1961 and June 1962. However, the airline's European network was mostly served by a fleet of eight turboprop Vickers Viscount 800s (from June 1957) and fifteen Lockheed L.188C Electras (from June 1959), until the introduction of DC-9-10s and -30s from March 1966 and November 1967 respectively. The piston fleet was gradually phased out, although four of the DC-7Cs had been converted for freight operations and remained in use until 1969. The Viscounts were sold to Aer Lingus in 1966, the Electras went to Universal Airlines between 1968 and 1969, and with the sale of the last Douglas DC-3 freighter in July 1970 KLM finally operated an all-jet fleet. By now the airline had also taken delivery of fourteen Douglas Super DC-8-63s, and went on to introduce Boeing 747-200Bs (from January 1971) and Douglas DC-10-30s (from December 1972).

Lockheed L.188C Electra PH-LLA illustrates the original two-tone blue colouring of KLM, with diagonal tail stripes and red titles and motifs. In later years the stripes were applied horizontally and the colouring of the titles etc. was changed to black. Then, prior to the introduction of the first Boeing 747s, the design illustrated by DC-8-55 PH-DCT was adopted, the tail now painted white to accommodate an enlarged KLM motif. In 1973 this was taken a step further by extending the upper pale blue cheatline over the cabin roof, thereby creating a coloured background for white company titling - a feature that has been adopted by KLM aircraft ever since.

LAKER AIRWAYS

Laker Airways was formed by Freddie Laker in February 1966 as a 'contract carrier to the package holiday trade' and commenced operations in July of that year using two Bristol Britannia 102s. Airline ownership was nothing new to Mr. Laker, as he had owned two airlines before they were merged with Airwork, Hunting-Clan and Silver City to form British United in 1960, when he became Managing Director of Britain's largest independent airline.

While with British United, Freddie Laker collaborated with BAC's design and engineering teams in drawing-up the specification for the One-Eleven (of which British United became the first operator), so this new aircraft was the obvious choice for his new airline. However, the One-Elevens were not the first aircraft to wear the black, red and white Laker livery (Mr. Laker's horse racing colours) because shortly after formation the company purchased two ex-BOAC Britannia 102s. These were introduced on charter work at the beginning of July 1966, but purely on an ad-hoc basis.

The first of three ordered BAC 1-11-300s was delivered at the end of February 1967 and, following the arrival of a second aircraft, entered service in April. The 1-11s were chiefly used on holiday charters to Spain and Italy, but because of the longer range of this particular model (over 1,800 miles), non-stop flights were also made to the Eastern Mediterranean, North Africa and the Canary Islands. An agreement had already been reached to lease the third aircraft to Air Congo prior to its delivery in May. This eventually entered service with Laker a year later, to coincide with the introduction of a fourth 1-11-300 for the 1968 summer season. In January of that year Laker also purchased the prototype VC-10, but prior to its delivery a fifteen-month lease was arranged with Middle East Airlines, after which it was immediately sold to British United. The Britannias remained in use until January 1969 when they were sold to Angkasa Civil Air Transport of Indonesia. In February of that year

Laker Airways added long-haul operations to its expanding services by taking over the lease of two Boeing 707-120Bs from British Eagle, which had ceased operations. These aircraft (G-AWDG illustrated) eventually entered service on transatlantic group charter flights from Gatwick, Manchester and Prestwick to New York and Toronto, while also supplementing the 1-11s on the European inclusive-tour work. The Boeing 707s were also used on services between Luxembourg and Barbados (via Gatwick) on behalf of International Caribbean Airways, which had been formed in September 1970 as a subsidiary company.

Laker first applied to operate transatlantic schedules from Gatwick in 1971, although approval was not forthcoming until two years later and then on the condition that Stansted Airport was used. In the meantime the airline had taken delivery of two McDonnell Douglas DC-10-10s in October/November 1972 which it had intended to use on a proposed walk on/no reservation service to the United States. The US authorities were also slow in approving the service and so the DC-10s found new employment, operating advance booking charters across the North Atlantic as well as high density IT flights to the major European holiday centres. The DC-10s were named 'Belles' in the tradition of some of the finest British railway trains, the first two being named 'Eastern Belle' and 'Western Belle' to reflect the transatlantic services planned for them, the special 'Skytrain' motif also incorporating portions of the British and American flags (as illustrated by G-BBSZ). Laker eventually operated a fleet of four DC-10-10s and five DC-10-30s, and also ordered ten Airbus Industrie A300B4s for use on proposed low fare European 'Skytrain' services. However, Laker's plans to revolutionise European air travel were firmly opposed and the airline, having taken delivery of the first three Airbus aircraft, eventually ceased all operations in early 1982.

LEBANESE INTERNATIONAL AIRWAYS

Lebanese International Airways was founded by Carlos and Alphonse Arida and commenced operations in January 1956 over a modest international network from Beirut. With technical and operational assistance from Sabena, operations were soon expanded and in June 1958 the airline leased a Douglas DC-6 from the Belgian carrier, registered OD-ACY. In 1963 LIA acquired three Douglas DC-7Cs from American Airlines, although one of these was sold to Alia (in which the Arida brothers held a financial interest) during the following year. By 1965 Lebanese International Airways was operating twice weekly schedules to Milan and Paris using chartered Boeing 720s, as well as regional services to Teheran, Kuwait, Baghdad, Bahrain and Doha.

Lebanese International introduced its own jet equipment in October 1966 when it purchased the first of two Convair 990s from American Airlines (OD-AEW illustrated). The second aircraft was delivered two years later but was only operated by the airline for two months. On December 28th 1968 an Israeli commando attack on Beirut Airport damaged the airline's Convair 990 and Douglas DC-7 fleets beyond economical repair, effectively bringing operations to an end. The traffic rights of Lebanese International Airways were subsequently acquired by Middle East Airlines (MEA) during the summer of 1969.

LOFTLEIDIR ICELANDIC AIRLINES

Loftleidir Icelandic Airlines was formed on March 10th 1944 by three young Icelandic pilots with the support of local businessmen. Operations began on April 7th with a seaplane service linking Reykjavik with various other communities within Iceland. Within a few years the airline was serving Copenhagen with Douglas DC-4 equipment, and on August 25th 1948 a regular service between Reykjavik and New York was opened.

From March 1952 Loftleidir confined its activities to the operation of low fare North Atlantic services linking New York and Reykjavik to Glasgow, London, Amsterdam, Luxembourg, Copenhagen, Gothenburg, Stavanger, Oslo and Helsinki, although all flights east of Iceland had IATA agreed fares. A fleet of five Douglas DC-6Bs was later supplemented by five turboprop Canadair CL-44s, delivered from May 1964. Known as 'Rolls Royce 400s' in Loftleidir service, the aircraft were configured to seat 189 economy-class passengers following modification to CL-44J standard, which involved increasing the fuselage length by 15ft.

Loftleidir entered the jet age during the summer of 1970 by leasing two Douglas DC-8-63CFs from Seaboard World. By this time the Douglas DC-6Bs had been phased out and the CL-44 fleet reduced by the transfer of one aircraft to Cargolux, in which Loftleidir held a financial interest. The airline continued to lease additional DC-8s from Seaboard World (N8641 illustrated), mainly on a seasonal basis, as the remaining CL-44s were made available to Cargolux. Loftleidir merged with Icelandair on August 1st 1973 and finally ceased to exist in 1979.

LOT POLISH AIRLINES

LOT was formed by the Polish Government on January 1st 1929 to take over the operations of the private companies Aerolot and Aero. Aerolot had opened scheduled services between Warsaw, Gdansk and Lwow as early as September 5th 1922 under the name of Polska Linia Lotnicza-Aerolloyd, whilst Aero-Komunikacja Powietrzna had operated a Warsaw-Poznan route since 1925. Soon after the formation, a competition was held to find an insignia for the new company. This competition was won by a young artist, Tadeusz Gronowski, who designed an emblem in the shape of a stylised crane in flight, enclosed in a circle. This symbol has been carried on all LOT aircraft ever since. The new airline improved its domestic services and built up a considerable international network, reaching as far north as Helsinki and southwards to Lydda in Palestine. However, the airline suffered a severe setback when all its equipment and ground installations were lost at the beginning of World War Two.

The company was re-activated on March 6th 1945 and, with the help of the Polish Air Force, resumed operations between Warsaw, Poznan and Szczecin on April 1st - using Lisunov Li-2s flown by the Seventh Independent Civil Aviation Squadron. When the war finally ended, some of LOT's pre-war personnel gradually began to return and in 1946 it was at last possible for the company to re-establish its pre-war international network, beginning with a Warsaw-Berlin connecting on May 11th, with Paris, Stockholm and Prague following in quick succession. Nine Douglas DC-3s were acquired and these were joined by five SE.161 Languedocs with accommodation for thirty-three passengers and, from April 1949, by five Ilyushin Il-12Bs. In the period between 1950 and 1955 the airline turned its attention towards establishing air connections with other East European countries and was instrumental in establishing the 'Pool of Six' (later known as the association of companies within the 'Warsaw Agreement') set up to provide a common system of air transport between the capitals of the Socialist countries. This agreement resulted in the opening of a route to Sofia in 1953, followed two years later by a Warsaw-Moscow service, with another connection to Moscow through Vilnius soon after. Vienna was added to the network at the same time.

In 1955 Ilyushin Il-14s were introduced on the airline's main trunk routes and gradually replaced the Il-12Bs, which were retired in 1959. From 1956 there was a considerable increase in economic contacts between Poland and the western world, and as a result LOT extended its activities to more distant routes. A new service was opened in 1957 to Athens which in the summer season was extended to include Belgrade and Tirana. A year later London and Zurich were added, followed by services to Amsterdam and Rome. Five Convair 240s were introduced to supplement the Il-14s on these routes.

The introduction into service on May 24th 1961 of LOT's first turboprop aircraft, the Ilyushin Il-18V (SP-LSE illustrated), ushered in a new era for the airline. This aircraft, with twice the speed and three times the range of the previous piston-engined types, enabled LOT to greatly increase its European services and to open new routes to the Middle East and Africa. Three Viscount 800s, acquired in 1962, initially supplemented these aircraft, and longer range Il-18Ds (SP-LSF illustrated) were added from November 1965. On April 20th 1966 LOT introduced the Antonov An-24 to its domestic and regional network, and then entered the jet era on November 5th 1968 with the delivery of the first of five Tupolev Tu-134 short haul jets, which aided further expansion of the airline's international route network

From March 1972 the airline steadily built up a fleet of Ilyushin Il-62s, which opened new services to the United States and Canada and also provided additional capacity on some of the more densely travelled routes to Europe. The original Il-62s were later replaced by the longer range Il-62M, delivered from April 1979, while the Il-18s were relegated to charter work - with some converted to supplement a small fleet of ex-Polish Air Force Antonov An-12 freighters operated from 1970.

MALEV HUNGARIAN AIRLINES

Malev was originally established on April 26th 1946 as a joint Hungarian/Soviet undertaking with the title of Maszovlet, using a fleet of eleven Lisunov Li-2s and six Polikarpov Po-2s. The present name was adopted on November 25th 1954 when the Soviet Union's 50% holding reverted to the Hungarian State. The original fleet of Li-2s was increased with the addition of a further fourteen in 1955, all of which had been retired from service by 1964. Malev is also known to have operated a large fleet of VEB-built Ilyushin Il-14s, eight of which remained in use at the start of the seventies.

The first of eight turboprop Ilyushin Il-18s was added in 1961 and enabled the inauguration of new services further afield. The Il-18s were used extensively on services throughout East and West Europe, and to the Middle East. Malev received its first jet equipment in December 1968, becoming one of the first export customers for the original 64-seat Tupolev Tu-134, while also acquiring the lengthened Tu-134A model in later years. Tupolev Tu-154s slowly began to replace Il-18s on scheduled passenger services from September 1973, relegating them to secondary routes and charter activities until their only useful purpose was to serve as freighters.

The original Malev livery, as worn by the Li-2s from 1954, was based on that of its predecessor, Maszovlet, with changes made to the cheatline colouring and titles. Malev took the opportunity to update its image with the arrival of its first Il-18s at the start of the 'sixties. The Hungarian flag was extended across the entire width of the fin where it was met by a stylised 'M' initial in pale blue. The cheatline was also changed for a more intricate design which involved wrapping the initial 'M' around the cockpit windows (illustrated by HA-MOA). The next livery change was also to coincide with the introduction of a new type, the Tupolev Tu-134, which again used the 'M' initial but in a more conventional manner. This design also welcomed the Tupolev Tu-154 to Malev's fleet in later years and was adopted by the remaining IL-18s from March 1975.

MARTINAIR HOLLAND

Martinair Holland, known until April 1968 as Martin's Air Charter, was formed on May 24th 1958 and initially undertook ad hoc and executive charters, aerial advertising and sightseeing flights with a de Havilland Dove. These initial activities were soon expanded following the introduction of Douglas DC-3 (and later DC-4 and DC-6) aircraft. By the summer of 1964 the company had absorbed two smaller Dutch operators, namely Veen's Air Services (in 1962) and Rotterdam-based Fairways (in January 1964), and subsequently a 25% shareholding was acquired by KLM.

With the Dutch national carrier now involved the airline was re-organised and long-haul charters were undertaken from October 1962 using an ex-KLM Douglas DC-7C. At this point Martin's Air Charter adopted a new livery based on the existing KLM design but with the pale blue colouring overpainted in red. Another three DC-7Cs were transferred to Martinair by the summer of 1965 and a smaller Convair 440 was acquired to undertake short to medium haul charters (later replaced by a turboprop Cv-600).

Jet operations began in June 1967 with the lease of a Douglas DC-8-33 from KLM, and as part of this modernisation programme the airline's name was changed to Martinair Holland. The first of three convertible Douglas DC-9-30s arrived in July 1968 and the remaining Douglas DC-7Cs were put up for sale at the end of the summer season. The airline also purchased a DC-8-55 from Overseas National which, like the DC-9s, could be configured for passenger or freight operations. Martinair finally operated an all-jet fleet on passenger services from October 1969, when a Fokker F.28-1000 Fellowship was acquired to replace the Convair 600.

The livery illustrated by DC-9-30 PH-MAX was an interim scheme based on the original red and blue colouring of Martin's Air Charter but with 'Martinair Holland' titles. This was later changed to coincide with the delivery of the company's first McDonnell Douglas DC-10-30 in November 1973.

MONARCH AIRLINES

Monarch Airlines was formed in June 1967 when Cosmos Tours decided to establish its own airline to operate inclusive tour services to holiday resorts in the Mediterranean. Luton Airport was selected as a base and the airline commenced operations on April 5th 1968 using two Bristol Britannia 312 aircraft acquired from Caledonian Airways. The airline operation of Cosmos was not restricted to flying holidaymakers and another source of revenue for Monarch was the undertaking of contract trooping charters for the Ministry of Defence. By 1970 another eight Britannias were operational, with another being purchased for spares. Most of these were obtained from the receivers of the sadly bankrupt British Eagle, including G-AOVN (illustrated). Monarch Airlines continued to fly its IT services and trooping flights with the Britannias until December 1971, when it introduced the first of four Boeing 720s.

The Britannias were gradually retired, the final passenger flight by one of these aircraft taking place in October 1974 when G-AOVT flew a London-Lisbon service for British Airways. In the meantime the Boeing 720s (G-AZFB illustrated) were busy earning their keep, and like the turboprop aircraft before them also flew some long range charters, including some carrying pilgrims to Mecca. One long haul charter flown regularly was a weekly service from Birmingham to Toronto and Vancouver, operated during the summer of 1974 on behalf of a Midlands-based travel company. However, by mid-August the service had been suspended following difficulties experienced by the travel company in arranging the trips.

Monarch was well aware that the large and fuel thirsty Boeing 720s were not the ideal aircraft for all its inclusive-tour flying. A smaller aircraft was desirable for those routes where traffic levels were lower. With the withdrawal of the Britannias Monarch turned to the BAC 1-11 to solve this problem, taking delivery of three used series -500 aircraft during 1975. As new resorts developed further from home the airline introduced a small fleet of Boeing 707-120s, which supplemented the '720 fleet from February 1978. By the late 'seventies these were being used on non-stop services to Crete and Las Palmas etc. in addition to routes between Luton and St. Lucia (via the Azores).

The fleet combination of both short and long-haul types was an ideal one, but Monarch became increasingly aware that neither the 1-11 or '720/707 were the most fuel efficient aircraft available. Fuel costs were high, and the age of the fleet was also beginning to cause some technical problems as it had with the Britannias ten years earlier. Consequently, the company decided to re-equip its entire fleet. The 1-11s would be replaced by Boeing 737-200 aircraft and the 720s by the new Boeing 757 twinjet. This was a very bold move for Monarch, but a decision made possible thanks to its sound financial backing from Cosmos. The decision to undertake this major re-equipment programme was announced in 1980, and with the first '757s in March 1983 came a revised livery.

National Airlines, known until July 8th 1937 as National Airlines System, was founded in St. Petersburg (Florida) and began air mail services on October 15th 1934 between St. Petersburg and Daytona Beach (via Tampa, Lakeland and Orlando) with two Ryan monoplanes. As these operations were expanded so larger Lockheed L.10 Electras and later Lodestars were added. The airline was awarded a route between Miami and New York in 1944 and operated it initially with Lodestars until Douglas DC-4s were introduced in February 1946 to provide the first non-stop service between the two cities. A further improvement occurred the following year when Douglas DC-6s were introduced and National inaugurated the 1093-mile over-water (Great Circle) route between Miami and New York, reducing the flight time from five to four hours. Lodestars continued to operate some of the multiple-stop services on this route until eventually replaced by Convair 340s in 1953.

The company's headquarters were moved from Jacksonville to Miami in 1946 and also in that year a service was opened to Havana, Cuba (later suspended in 1960 for political reasons). Further improvements were made on the Miami-New York route in 1952 with the introduction of DC-6Bs, in 1953 with DC-7s and in 1957 with DC-7Bs and Lockheed Super Constellations (N7133C illustrated), but the big improvement came in December 1958 when National Airlines became the first US domestic airline to introduce jets. This was achieved at such an early date by leasing Boeing 707s from Pan American, which had introduced them on services to Europe in October of that year. The aircraft retained their Pan Am livery because they operated the two and a half hour New York-Miami flights between transatlantic trips. Turboprop Lockheed Electras were introduced in 1959 and National started forming its own jet fleet in 1960 with the arrival of its first Douglas DC-8-20s.

Another big event in the history of National Airlines occured in 1961, when it was awarded the Southern trans-continental route between Florida and California. The Western boundary of the route network, which had been extended to Houston (Texas) in 1956, was suddenly pushed some 1,500 miles to the west coast to include Los Angeles, San Diego and San Francisco (plus Las Vegas en route). This brought the airline's unduplicated route mileage up to 12,345 miles and provided an extensive network which linked major cities on the Atlantic, Gulf and Pacific coasts.

At this time the airline's livery was a pale blue cheatline with red flashes and pale blue stars on the nose and fin, the stars supporting the legend 'Airline of the Stars' on the fuselage. The stars and legend were later dropped to leave a simplified livery in the same colours. In 1963 National became the first US domestic airline to operate an all turbine-powered fleet, comprising turboprop Electras and turbojet DC-8s. Then, in 1964, the first of the Boeing 727s began to arrive and the number of these increased through the following years - first with the short-fuselage version and later the stretched -200 - until, in 1968, the airline was able to sell its Electras and become an all-jet operator.

A major image change occured in 1967 when the new yellow and orange livery (illustrated) was introduced. Then, in 1970, National Airlines inaugurated transatlantic services between Miami and London, initially using two Douglas DC-8-50s leased from Airlift. These were later replaced by two 370-seat Boeing 747-100s, although National subsequently selected the McDonnell Douglas DC-10-30 for its transatlantic network, later extended to Paris, Frankfurt, Zurich and Amsterdam, while the DC-10-10 was chosen to replace DC-8-50s and -61s used on domestic trunk routes. National Airlines merged with Pan American on January 7th 1980 and its fleet was gradually repainted to wear the livery of this airline.

National Airlines

NORTHEAST AIRLINES

Northeast Airlines was created on November 1st 1970 when BKS Air Transport finally lost its long standing identity to a new family image designed for the regional subsidiaries of British European Airways. The same basic livery was adopted by Northeast Airlines and Cambrian Airways in yellow and orange respectively, complimented by black titles and motifs. The operations of Cambrian and BKS remained, however, basically unchanged.

The Tridents and Britannias flew the scheduled routes and inclusive tour charters from Newcastle while the Viscounts operated solely from Leeds. International routes from London were also serviced by the Trident fleet. The remaining Britannias were phased out in 1971 following the introduction of an ex-Channel Airways Trident 1E.

Northeast Airlines was to lose its identity in October 1973, after which its fleet of Viscounts and Tridents displayed British Airways titling and were gradually repainted to wear the national carrier's full red, white and blue livery. The only concession to Northeast's own existence was small company titling carried on the lower forward fuselage in white, with this too disappearing in 1976. The last aircraft to operate under the Northeast callsign was Trident 1E G-AVYB, which flew service NS.458 from Newcastle to Heathrow on the evening of March 31st 1973.

PACIFIC WESTERN AIRLINES

Pacific Western Airlines, known until May 15th 1953 as Central British Columbia Airways, was founded at Fort. St. James on July 1st 1945. Its activities consisted entirely of contract charter work until 1953, when a scheduled service was opened from Vancouver to Kitimat, following the acquisition of Associated Air Taxi Ltd. The airline improved and strengthened its operations considerably over the years through the purchase of many small companies. By 1965, Pacific Western was ranked Canada's third largest airline, and operated an extensive network of scheduled and non-scheduled services throughout British Columbia, Alberta, Saskatchewan and the Northwest Territories with a forty-seven strong fleet, including two Douglas DC-7C, two Douglas DC-6, two DC-6B, two DC-4, four DC-3, three Curtiss C-46 Commando, two Beech 18, fourteen DHC-2 Beaver, six DHC-3 Otter and two Grumman Goose aircraft. The larger DC-6s were used on 'Air Bus' services between Edmonton and Calgary, which had been inaugurated in 1963, while the DC-7Cs were employed to operate international charters. In May 1967 Pacific Western acquired a Lockheed L.100-20 Hercules freighter to expand its cargo charter activities both at home and abroad. The fleet was later increased to three aircraft and within the first three years of Hercules operations Pacific Western flew into fifty-two different countries in the free world. The domestic fleet was modernised with the introduction of turboprop Convair 640s (from February 1967) and later Boeing 737-200s (from November 1968). Two Boeing 727-100Cs were added in October 1972 and February 1974, while two Boeing 707-120Bs (later one 707-120B and one -320C) were acquired for the long-haul charter operations, which included a regular programme of holiday flights to London-Gatwick.

Pacific Western later joined forces with CP Air to form Canadian Airlines International on April 26th 1987, by which time its fleet had been standardised on Boeing 737 equipment. The livery illustrated by L.100-30 C-GHPW was adopted during the mid-seventies to succeed a similar but less colourful design, and was modernised again at the start of the 'eighties.

Overseas National Airways was originally founded in June 1950 and commenced operations with a fleet of five Douglas DC-4s, primarily flying under contract to the United States Air Force in connection with the Korean war. The airline was inactive for a period of two years from October 1963, during which time it was extensively re-organised. When operations re-commenced in October 1965 Overseas National operated a fleet of seven Douglas DC-7s, including two DC-7C/Fs, on both commercial and military charter work. Jet operations were inaugurated following the delivery of two new Douglas DC-8-50Fs in June and July 1966, which triggered major expansion of the company's fleet and activities. Between 1967 and 1969 the airline took delivery of several new jetliners from the Douglas Aircraft Company, including seven DC-9-32s and two Super DC-8-63CFs, and also incorporated a fleet of eight Lockheed L.188A/F Electras. These were later joined by three ex-Eastern DC-8-20s (in 1973) and two ex-Spear Air DC-8-30s (in 1974), while the DC-8-61/63 fleet eventually peaked at seven aircraft in December 1973 following the addition of both new and used aircraft.

Overseas National was also an early customer for the Douglas DC-10-30CF, initially ordering three aircraft (plus three options) for delivery from April 1973. The first of these entered service on May 5th 1973 on the busy charter programme between Los Angeles and London-Gatwick; the second (N1032F illustrated) followed soon afterwards but the third was cancelled prior to delivery. The entire jet fleet could easily be configured to operate either passenger or freight charters as governed by demand. By now, the airline's activities included non-scheduled passenger and freight services within the United States and to the Caribbean, worldwide military charters, and transatlantic passenger charters - reaching as far east as India.

During 1974 the airline decided to paint one or more of its aircraft in a red, white and blue stars and stripes scheme in recognition of the USA's bi-centennial anniversary. The design initially chosen was created by Sharon Duker, an Overseas National cabin attendant, in an intra-company competition that attracted over one hundred entries. Two aircraft were eventually repainted, N1776R 'Independence' in the stars and stripes design and N1976P 'Dixie' in a scheme depicting the flag of the Confederate States (illustrated), the registrations reflecting the 200 year span of the United States (1776-1976). Between 1975 and 1977 the 'birthday card' liveries were seen throughout the United States, the Caribbean and Hawaii, and occasionally in Europe as well.

Tragedy struck during the winter of 1975/76 when the two DC-10s were lost, one at New York's Kennedy Airport in November 1975 and the other at Istanbul in January 1976. Losing both of these aircraft within the space of two months was a major blow to the airline, and Overseas National struggled to overcome the adverse publicity surrounding this unfortunate chain of events. Three more DC-10-30CFs were ordered for delivery from May 1977, following which most of the DC-8s were sold. The airline eventually ceased operations during the summer of 1978 and the DC-10-30s were remarketed by Seaboard World Airlines.

PAN AMERICAN WORLD AIRWAYS

Pan American World Airways was originally organised on March 14th 1927 to bid for the air mail contract between Key West (Florida) and Havana (Cuba), the first flight over this ninety mile route taking place on October 19th with a chartered Fairchild floatplane. From these very humble beginnings the airline soon expanded its operations throughout the Caribbean and Latin America, swallowing up many smaller carriers along the way. On February 25th 1929 Pan Am joined with the W.R. Grace steamship interests in the formation of Pan American-Grace Airways (Panagra), to operate along South America's west coast and across the Andes to Buenos Aires. Services over the Pacific and Atlantic oceans followed and through a number of shrewd purchase and pool arrangements Pan American went on to become one of the most influential airlines in the world, with a network spanning all continents. A major event in the history of Pan Am took place on October 26th 1958, when it became the first airline to put the original turbojet Boeing 707-120 into operation, introducing the type on its daily New York-London schedule. These aircraft were soon replaced by 707-320Bs on long-haul routes which, together with Douglas DC-8-30s, began to replace piston-engined aircraft such as Stratocruisers and Douglas DC-7s, relegating the latter to cargo operations. In 1965 the airline ordered eleven Boeing 727-100s to replace DC-6Bs on its internal German and Caribbean routes, and in April 1966 followed this with an order for twenty-three all-passenger Boeing 747s and two freighters. Once again, Pan American led the way into this new era of air transport, introducing the first 'jumbo jets' on its New York-London route on January 22nd 1970.

The livery illustrated by Douglas DC-6B N6106C, seen at San Francisco in June 1958, was designed for the new fleet of jet aircraft (which had been ordered in October 1955), and remained the standard colouring of Pan American (later Pan Am) until the cheatline finally disappeared from the design in 1984. Despite these refinements, the traditional tail motif remained in use until the company ceased operations on December 4th 1991, following years of financial instability.

PIA (PAKISTAN INTERNATIONAL AIRLINES

Pakistan International Airlines was formed in 1951 as a Government department, and began operations on June 7th 1954 when a fleet of three newly-delivered Lockheed L-1049C Super Constellations opened a valuable link between East and West Pakistan. International routes to Cairo and London followed on February 1st 1955 and the name Pakistan International Airlines Corporation was adopted on March 10th of that year, when the operations of Orient Airways were absorbed. Founded on October 23rd 1946, prior to the partitioning of India, Orient Airways had established a network of scheduled services within, and between East and West Pakistan.

The airline took delivery of three new Viscount 800s between January and March 1959, but lost two of these aircraft almost immediately and had to wait for replacements to arrive in August and September before earlier Convair 240s could be replaced. As it happens, these were traded-in to Fokker in October 1959 against the purchase of new F-27 Friendships, which started to arrive from January 1961. The corporation was responsible for the operation of all services within Pakistan, including helicopter and 'Air Bus' services (the former using three Sikorsky S.61Ns), and regional services to Bombay, Delhi, Calcutta, Kathmandu, Rangoon and Kabul. The first jet aircraft to be introduced by PIA was the Boeing 720B (in December 1961), and by 1965 four of these were in use and services to London had been increased to six-times-weekly, flown via Teheran, Beirut, Rome, Geneva, Moscow and Frankfurt. Four Trident 1Es were acquired from March 1966 to replace the Viscounts in regional use, while long-haul modernisation and expansion was left to a fleet of Boeing 707-320Cs, introduced from July 1966 (AP-AWU illustrated). In later years PIA added Douglas DC-10-30s (from February 1974) and new and used 747-200s (from April 1976), and eventually replaced the earlier 720Bs with 737-300s from May 1985.

QANTAS

Qantas can trace its history back to 1920 when Queensland and Northern Territory Aerial Services was founded on November 16th. On November 2nd 1922. Non-scheduled and taxi flights were initially operated and on November 2nd 1922 the airline opened its first regular service, between Charleville and Cloncurry, with Armstrong Whitworth FK.8 biplanes. A new company, Qantas Empire Airways Ltd., was organised in conjunction with Imperial Airways on January 18th 1934, to fly the Brisbane-Singapore sector of the England-Australia service, known as the 'Kangaroo' route. Through-services to London were started on December 1st 1947 (with Lockheed L-749 Constellations). A trans-Pacific network was established in April 1954 (between Sydney, Fiji, Honolulu, San Francisco and Vancouver), and on January 14th 1958 Qantas became the first airline to operate round-the-world services through San Francisco and New York (with Lockheed Super Constellations).

The livery illustrated by Boeing 707-320C VH-EBN was the last of four designs adopted by the type during its career with the Australian airline. The original turbojet '707-120s (introduced from July 1959) were painted to wear an existing scheme, based on a BOAC-style livery but with red cheatlines and tail stripes. Next was the V-Jet design, which came with the first turbofan 707-120Bs in July 1961; the V originating from the latin word 'Vannus' or fan. The third revision involved the titling, which was changed from 'Qantas-Australia's Overseas Airline' to 'Qantas-Australia' in 1970, and the fourth came as a result of the introduction of Boeing 747-200Bs during the summer of 1971, when the traditional 'winged kangaroo' motif was expanded to become the livery's centrepiece and the cheatline colouring was changed to orange.

ROUSSEAU AVIATION

Rousseau Aviation commenced flying in July 1963 with a single Douglas DC-3 and initiated scheduled operations three years later over the route Lannion-Saint Brieuc-Paris, which was flown in collabora-tion with Air Inter. By 1970 the fleet had grown to include two Hawker Siddeley (Avro) 748s, eight Nord 262s and four Douglas DC-3s, and during that year the airline carried 193,458 passengers over a network spanning Dinard, Jersey, St. Brieuc, Quimper, London (Gatwick), Lannion, Paris (Orly), Lille, Metz and Mulhouse. In addition, Dinard, Rennes, Nancy, Nantes, Bordeaux and Clermont Ferrand were served in conjunction with Air Inter using Nord 262s painted in dual Rousseau/Air Inter markings. Routes along the Normandy and Brittany coasts were flown mainly during the summer season. The airline also operated charters to destinations in Europe, the Middle East and North Africa, and employed a small fleet single and twin engined aircraft - primarily for charter and air-taxi work from its base at Aerodrome de Dinard-Pleurtuit.

The basic livery of Rousseau Aviation, as illustrated by Douglas DC-3 F-BAXR, was similar in style and colouring to that of Air France, from whom Rousseau had purchased its original DC-3 fleet, but with 'RA' initials added to the tail insignia. This livery was also adopted by the Nord 262 and HS-748 aircraft. When Rousseau Aviation's parent, SASMAT (Societe Auxiliare de Services et de Materiel Aeronautiques), took control of Touraine Air Transport (TAT) in 1973 it was decided to merge the operations of these airlines, together with those of Air Paris and Taxi Avia France, to form one major regional carrier. The HS-748s and remaining Nord 262s were therefore repainted to wear full TAT markings, which emerged as the surviving airline.

SAGITTAIR

Sagittair was formed in late 1969 with the intention of operating inclusive-tour passenger charters to the ski resorts of Switzerland and Austria using a fleet of Beech 18s. However, instead of flying holidaymakers, the airline's first revenue flight left London (Heathrow) for Geneva with a cargo of newspapers. This flight took place on May 27th 1970 and shaped the general pattern of the airline's future activities. Cargo charter operations from Heathrow became so popular that the airline 'moved in' and established its own engineering facilities and operations office at the airport. In 1971 Saggitair applied to operate scheduled cargo flights from East Midlands and Heathrow to Beaveaus using Douglas DC-3 or DC-6 aircraft, and to Lille with Argosy equipment. Both routes were approved but in the meantime the airline had decided to standardise its fleet on the Argosy (G-APRN illustrated). Two aircraft were initially purchased from Universal Airlines of the United States, joining the fleet in April and August 1971.

Twice-weekly services between East Midlands and Lille were inaugurated on November 9th, and a service to Guernsey soon followed. The three Beech 18s were phased out during the winter months and a third Argosy arrived in January 1972. In addition to the scheduled services, Sagittair also operated numerous ad-hoc charter flights with the Argosy aircraft, and the sighting of operations at East Midlands became permanent. Financial problems began to appear in May 1972 and although a subsequent dock strike created a flurry of work between July and August, ongoing financial problems finally led to the airline's closure on September 8th.

SATURN AIRWAYS

Saturn Airways was founded in 1948 as All-American Airways and was engaged primarily in domestic military passenger charter operations using Curtiss C-46 aircraft. The name Saturn Airways was adopted in 1960 as the company began to develop its civil passenger charter business, aided by the introduction of DC-6Bs that year and Douglas DC-7s from 1963. In 1964 Saturn was awarded a five year certificate by the CAB to perform trans Atlantic passenger charters, initially with DC-6B equipment and later with 104-passenger DC-7C aircraft. Further expansion took place in 1965 when the airline merged with Aaxico Airlines, which had been engaged exclusively in military contract work since 1945.

During the winter of 1967/68 Saturn took delivery of two Douglas DC-8-61s, which assumed all trans Atlantic and commercial charter operations. Further expansion followed during the early 'seventies as older piston-engined aircraft were replaced by a large fleet of Lockheed Hercules freighters, and following the collapse of Universal Airlines in May 1972 these were joined by nine L.188CF Electras. By then, Saturn was operating passenger charters to Europe, Africa and parts of Asia, in addition to passenger and freight services within the United States and to the Caribbean. The airline also held exemption authority to carry outsize loads virtually anywhere in the world. Oakland-based Saturn Airways was acquired by the Transamerica Corporation on December 1st 1976 and its operations and fleet were absorbed by Trans International Airlines.

The airline's livery is illustrated by Boeing 707-320C N763U, one of three ordered by Saturn but cancelled prior to delivery during the summer of 1968.

SAS (SCANDINAVIAN AIRLINES SYSTEM)

SAS was originally formed as OSAS on August 1st 1946 to operate the overseas services of the national airlines of Sweden, Norway and Denmark, namely SILA (Svensk Intercontinental Lufttraffik), DNL (Det Norske Luftfartselskap) and DDL (Det Danske Lifffartselskap), with the assets, aircraft and operations being divided in the ratio 3-2-2 respectively. The first flight under SAS auspices was undertaken on August 5th 1946 by a DNL Douglas DC-4, although there had not been time to paint the aircraft in the new livery. However, on September 17th a DDL DC-4, this time suitably painted for the occasion, took off from Bromma to inaugurate the first official westbound transatlantic service of the new organisation. A second route to Montevideo was opened on November 30th and later extended to Buenos Aires in April 1947. Meanwhile, DDL, DNL and ABA (Aktiebologet Aero Transport) continued to compete with each other on European routes, with mounting financial losses. Again protracted negotiations took place on this issue and, to overcome the prime obstacle created by having two separate Swedish carriers, SILA's interest was transferred to ABA on July 1st 1948 and the two companies were amalgamated. The new consortium (ESAS) had, infact, already begun operations on April 18th. Its combined fleet included an impressive thirty-nine Douglas DC-3s and eleven C-47s (for cargo flights). All aircraft, except a few operating on purely domestic routes, now carried SAS markings and were officially incorporated within the new fleet on August 1st 1948, although ownership and registration remained with the individual countries. A new long-haul route was opened by OSAS on October 26th 1949, linking Scandinavia with South East Asia over a seven-stop flight to Bangkok. On October 1st 1950 the operations of ABA, DDL, DNL, OSAS and ESAS were fully integrated, with SAS assuming all services and the original carriers acting merely as holding companies.

SAS established an early relationship with the Douglas Aircraft Company through the use of DC-3 and DC-4 aircraft, which developed further with the introduction of DC-6s (from April 1948), DC-6Bs (from May 1952) and DC-7Cs (from August 1956). The Douglas DC-3s were replaced by a large fleet of Convair 440s during the mid-'fifties, following an earlier evaluation of the Saab Scandia. On June 28th 1957 SAS ordered six Caravelle 1s (including one for Swissair) and inaugurated services with the type on April 26th 1959, between Scandinavia and the Middle East. For long haul services the airline once again turned to Douglas, taking delivery of seven DC-8-30s from March 1960. By early 1965 the fleet comprised eight DC-7Cs, one DC-7CF, twenty-two Caravelle 3s (including four leased to Swissair), nineteen Convair 440s, seven DC-8-30s and two Convair 990s (leased from Swissair). Two DC-8-50s were added in April 1965 and February 1966 (when the leased Cv-990s were returned), and in later years the airline introduced DC-8-62s (from May 1967) and DC-8-63s (from August 1968). In 1967 some DC-9-30s were leased from Swissair and SAS subsequently decided to standardise on the Douglas airliner. The aircraft ordered by SAS were tailored-made for its requirements, the DC-9-20 for domestic operations and the series-40 for short to medium haul use. The former utilised the short body of the DC-9-10 but with the longer wingspan and more powerful engines of the DC-9-30 series, while the DC-9-40 came with a modest fuselage stretch offering increased accommodation for 125 passengers - entering service with SAS on March 12th 1968. The remaining Caravelles were finally phased-out in 1974, by which time SAS had taken delivery of fifty DC-9s (forty DC-9-40s and ten DC-9-20s).

The illustrated livery was also applied to three wide-bodied types, namely Boeing 747-200Bs (from February 1971), Douglas DC-10-30s (from October 1974) and Airbus Industrie A300B2/B4s (from January 1980), before the current design was adopted in 1983.

SABENA - BELGIAN WORLD AIRLINES

Sabena was formed on May 23rd 1923 to succeed the Syndicat National pour l'Etide de Transports Aeriens (SNETA), which had been established three years earlier to create air routes to neighbouring European countries and a separate network within the Belgian Congo. By 1938 Sabena's European routes penetrated Germany, the Netherlands, Scandinavia, France, Czechoslovakia, Austria and the United Kingdom, and there was a also a weekly Belgium-Congo service flown with Savoia-Marchetti S.83s. From 1940 operations were conducted solely in Africa and for four years Sabena aircraft carried men and materials in support of the war effort.

The airline resumed European services after the war and by October 1946 the fleet had grown to twenty-eight aircraft, including nine Douglas DC-3s and four DC-4s, and in that year nineteen additional aircraft were ordered, including three Douglas DC-6s, two more DC-4s and eight DC-3s; some de Havilland Doves were also purchased and in 1949 the Convair 240 was introduced. The network soon covered most of Europe, extending eastwards into the Middle East, north as far as Stockholm, south to Johannesburg and west to three ports of call on the American continent.

In September 1953 Sabena opened the world's first international passenger-carrying helicopter service, which linked the city centre of Brussels with Lille, Maastricht and Rotterdam, and also with Antwerp and Liege, using Sikorsky S.55s. In later years the service was extended to Cologne, Bonn, Dortmund, Eindhoven, Duisburg and Paris. In 1957 the S.55s were replaced by eight S.58s, which had accommodation for twelve passengers. By the end of 1960 the helicopters had carried 300,000 passengers and amassed 62,000 flying hours. The helicopter operations were gradually scaled down as conventional airport-to-airport services improved. In the meantime, Sabena had acquired a fleet of eleven DC-6Bs (from 1953), twelve Convair 440s (between June and December 1956) and ten DC-7Cs (from November 1956). During the summer of 1958 the airline also leased two Lockheed L-1049H Super Constellations from Seaboard and Western Airlines to provide additional capacity during the Brussels Trade Fair, both of which displayed full Sabena markings.

The airline ordered its first jet equipment in December 1955 when it signed for five Boeing 707-320s (later increased to seven) for delivery from December 1959. Sabena was the first European airline to introduce Boeing 707s, which entered service on its African and transatlantic routes and also extended the long-haul network to Mexico. In addition, eight Caravelle 6Ns were added between January and August 1961 to replace Convair 440s and Douglas DC-6s used on its European network, and on services to the Middle East. Sabena went on to add another two Caravelles (by April 1965), seven '707-320Cs (between April 1965 and December '69), five Boeing 727-100/Cs (from April 1967), one Fokker F.27-600 (in August 1969), two 747-100s (from December 1970) and three Douglas DC-10-30CFs (from August 1973).

The livery illustrated by Convair 440 OO-SCV was adopted prior to the delivery of the first Boeing 707s, the most significant change from the previous design (illustrated by Douglas DC-6B OO-CTP) being the introduction of a large white 'S' motif over a blue coloured fin, which in different styles has been carried by all Sabena aircraft ever since. The livery remained in use until the summer of 1973, during which time it was adopted by all aircraft operated - ranging from Douglas DC-3s to the first Boeing 747-100s.

SEABOARD WORLD AIRLINES

Seaboard World Airlines was formed in September 1946 by two former USAAF pilots as Seaboard and Western Airlines. Irregular operations were started on May 10th 1947 using a single Douglas DC-4 on services to Europe. In 1949 the airline took part in the Berlin airlift and a year later, in July 1950, flew the first support flight from the United States for the United Nations Organisation in South Korea. The company was awarded a scheduled freight licence in June 1955 and inaugurated regular services between New York and Frankfurt on April 10th 1956. Seaboard and Western was substantially re-organised in 1960 and this was followed by a change of title to Seaboard World Airlines on April 26th 1961. In June of that year the airline received the first of seven ordered Canadair CL-44D4s, which entered service on July 25th between Frankfurt and New York. Jet operations were initiated three years later following the delivery of a new Douglas DC-8-50 freighter in June 1964, and for a while Seaboard operated a mixed fleet based on the original S & W Super Constellations, turboprop CL-44s and DC-8-50F equipment. A Curtiss C-46 Commando was also employed in support of the airline's European network, and displayed full Seaboard World markings. The airline originally placed an order for three Boeing 707-320Cs for delivery from February 1968, but later decided to standardise its fleet on the Douglas DC-8-63CF, incorporating twelve of these aircraft between June 1968 and October 1969. Subsequently, the first two '707-320Cs were sold to Varig soon after delivery and the third aircraft was cancelled.

The livery illustrated by Douglas DC-8-50F N8783R was based the original design, which featured smaller 'Seaboard World Airlines' titling. Following the introduction of the airline's first Boeing 747-200F 'Containership' in July 1974, the mustard tail colouring was incorporated within the cheatline as part of a totally new design, which remained in use until Seaboard World was taken over by Flying Tigers in December 1980.

SPEARAIR

Spearair was formed as a passenger charter airline and commenced operations following the purchase of two Douglas DC-8-30s from National Airlines during the winter of 1972/73. Kar Air, not to be overshadowed by this newcomer to the scene, responded by acquiring a DC-8-50 within a month of the first aircraft being delivered, and although Spearair managed to survive this initial clash of interests to successfully complete its first year of operations, its long term future was already in doubt. On August 5th 1974 the two DC-8s were repossessed by National Airlines and Spearair effectively ceased to exist.

Spearair's livery was both colourful and inventive, an unusual feature of the design being the prominent display of the company's motif over the rear fuselage and fin. The two aircraft were also individually coloured, using combinations of black and orange and black and burgundy, the latter illustrated by OH-SOB.

SOUTH AFRICAN AIRWAYS

South African Airways was established by the Union Government on February 1st 1934 as a subsidiary of South African Railways to take over the assets of Union Airways. Formed on August 28th 1929, Union Airways had provided a small network of services between Cape Town, Port Elizabeth, Durban and Johannesburg. The new airline began operations on February 1st 1934 with a fleet of single-engined Junkers F13s, later supplemented by a considerable number of Ju52/3Ms and Ju86s. South West African Airways was absorbed on February 1st 1935, adding Windhoek to its route system. Services to London were inaugurated in January 1946 with leased Avro Yorks, flown in association with BOAC. The airline's international network was expanded during the immediate post war years following the introduction of seven Douglas DC-4s (from March 1946), while eight Vickers Vikings were acquired (from October 1958) to improve domestic and regional links, supplemented by Douglas DC-3s. In June 1946 the 'springbok' service to London was upgraded to DC-4 equipment and flown three-times-monthly via Nairobi, Khartoum and Tripoli. The DC-4s were also used to establish links with other European capitals, supplemented by four Lockheed L-749A Constellations (ZS-DBR illustrated) from the summer of 1950. The Vikings were sold to British European Airways soon after, although the airline later returned to Vickers to order seven Viscount 800s for delivery between October 1958 and January 1959 - another being acquired from Cubana in 1962. South African Airways also took delivery of four Douglas DC-7Bs from February 1956.

Jet operations were started in the summer of 1960 when the airline took delivery of three Boeing 707-320s to replace the L-749As. By 1965 the airline's international network served Lisbon, Rome, Athens, Zurich, Frankfurt, Paris and London. There was also a once-fortnightly service between Johannesburg and Perth (Australia), which routed via Mauritius and the Cocos Islands. During that year the airline added the first of two ordered Boeing 707-320Bs and also took delivery of five 727-100s to replace the remaining Douglas DC-4s in regional use. The airline went on to acquire four 707-320Cs (from February 1968), six 737-200s (from October 1968) and three 747-200s (from October 1971), while the route network was extended to serve Brussels, Amsterdam, Geneva, Luxembourg, Madrid, Sydney, Rio de Janeiro, Buenos Aires and New York. An all-jet fleet fleet was finally reached with the sale of the Viscount 800 fleet to British Midland Airways in early 1972.

The original orange and blue colouring of South African Airways was introduced during 1960 with the delivery of the company's first Boeing 707. As with previous designs, the cheatline was blue and emanated from a winged springbok motif below the cockpit windows, while the tradition of applying titles in English and Afrikaanse on opposite sides of the fuselage was also retained - as it is today. An example of this is provided by L-749A ZS-DBR, which is seen prior to delivery in April 1950. With the introduction of the company's first Boeing 747-200 in November 1971 many of these post-war characteristics were finally removed from the design, the most significant change being the separation of the winged springbok from the forward cheatline arrangement, and the re-styling of the motif (illustrated by 747-200B ZS-SAO). The springbok was also separated from the blue and white tail flash and orange trim was added to the cheatline for the first time. Later applied to Boeing 747SPs (from March 1976) and Airbus A300B4s (from November 1976), the livery underwent further modernisation in creating the design in use today.

Spantax was founded on October 6th 1959 as Aero Taxis de Espana S.A. and commenced operations as a light charter and air-taxi operator. In due course, the airline was awarded a contract to undertake oil-drilling support operations in the Spanish Sahara region, which involved ferrying crews and equipment from Las Palmas. A Douglas DC-3 was soon acquired to supplement this operation, followed by two more during the latter part of 1960. The fledgling airline soon found plenty of work for its aircraft and by the end of 1960 had carried some 14,000 passengers on tourist charters within the Canary Islands.

Major expansion followed in 1962 when the airline doubled the size of its DC-3 fleet and also acquired three Douglas DC-4s from Iberia. Combined passenger and freight charters were initiated between Las Palmas and North Africa, and in October of that year a technical assistance agreement covering operations and equipment was concluded with Air Mauritanie. Charter and inclusive tour work was also undertaken, especially to and from the United Kingdom, in co-operation with the principle Spanish and foreign tour companies. As this work developed so the fleet was expanded, and by 1965 Spantax was operating seven Douglas DC-3s, four Douglas DC-4s, two DC-6s, three Douglas DC-7s and a Beech 18. The DC-4 fleet was increased to six units in 1966 and another two DC-7Cs were acquired, one from Alitalia and the other from Sabena. At the same time American Airlines was starting to dispose of its fleet of Convair 990As and Spantax, which had been considering the introduction of jet aircraft since early 1965, obliged by purchasing two of these aircraft for introduction during the summer of 1967. However, if this was to mark the end of piston-engined operations it certainly had no immediate effect. That same year Spantax added another DC-4 and also purchased the first of two DC-7CF freighters from Sabena, the second arriving in 1969.

It took several years for American Airlines to dispose of its fleet of Convair 990As, which enabled Spantax to phase-in more more of these aircraft as market conditions dictated, with another eight being acquired between 1968 and 1972. One of the most popular destinations for these aircraft was London-Gatwick, where it was possible to observe as many as four Cv-990 movements a day during the peak summer months of the 'seventies. The Douglas DC-4s and DC-7s were gradually phased-out from 1970, and those that remained in use from 1973 onwards were mostly configured for cargo operations. One of the Douglas DC-6s had received a swing-tail modification in earlier years to facilitate the loading and unloading of freight, and to accommodate loads that exceeded the dimensions of the standard side cargo door entrance. Only two Douglas DC-6s were converted as such, the other serving with Kar Air of Finland. In addition to general charters the airline also operated scheduled freight flights under contract to Iberia. In 1973 Spantax purchased two former Trans Caribbean Airways Douglas DC-8-61CFs from American Airlines, and in 1974 added two DC-9-14s (later increased to three) for lower-density IT operations. The Convair 990A fleet had by now suffered two losses, but its popularity within the airline remained as high as ever. It was therefore no surprise that when Swissair phased out its 'Coronados' in 1975, Spantax was only too happy to add another four of these high-performance machines to its fleet. As time went on the '990As became increasingly costly to operate, and with rising fuel costs, not to mention restraints on noise and polution, the airline found itself with a large, unsaleable fleet that urgently needed replacing. Some of these aircraft did remain in use until the point when Spantax finally ceased operations on March 29th 1988, although the majority were openly stored at Palma.

The pale blue and white livery of Spantax was unchanged for many years, although its application varied slightly on different types and some minor changes were made to the style and positioning of the titles, as illustrated by Douglas DC-6 EC-AZX and DC-7CF EC-BSP. In 1983 this was changed for a more colourful two-tone blue and orange design to coincide with the introduction of leased Boeing 737-200s. This revised livery was also adopted by the DC-8-61s and a few of the remaining Convair 990s, as well as Douglas DC-10 and MD-80 equipment in later years.

SWISSAIR

Swissair was founded on March 26th 1931 by the amalgamation of Ad Astra Aero AG and Basler Luftverkehr (known as Balair), which had operated Fokker F.V11B/3M's on services to France and Germany since April 12th 1926. Ad Astra Aero was formed on September 20th 1919 as Frick & Co. (renamed on December 15th), and acquired two other enterprises, Aero-Gesellschaft Comte, Mittelholzer & Co. and Avion-Tourisme Ltd. on February 24th and April 21st 1920 respectively. These pioneer companies engaged mainly in joy-riding and experimental flying until Ad Astra inaugurated scheduled services on June 1st 1922 between Geneva and Nuremburg. In the years that followed Swissair set many new standards in European air travel, becoming the first to employ stewardesses (in 1933) and the first in Europe to introduce the Douglas DC-2 into service, which inaugurated the route between Zurich, Basle and London in 1935. Swissair continued to build up a European network, but had to suspend all regular operations on the outbreak of the Second World War.

The airline resumed services to the United Kingdom, Belgium, Holland, France, Germany and Yugoslavia soon after the war, with Douglas DC-3s now forming the nucleus of its fleet. Early in 1949 Convair 240s were acquired and replaced the DC-3s on some of the longer European routes. The end of April 1949 also saw regular transatlantic flights by Douglas DC-4 aircraft between Switzerland and New York. These were later replaced by a small fleet of Douglas DC-6Bs (delivered from June 1951), while Convair 440s (introduced from 1955) became the standard equipment of European operations. Between November 1956 and 1958 the airline also acquired five Douglas DC-7Cs and increased its DC-6B fleet to eight units.

Swissair received its first Douglas DC-8 and Caravelle aircraft in April 1960, which enabled jet aircraft to be introduced to its long and short-haul networks at around the same time. The airline took delivery of three DC-8-30s and four Caravelle 3s that summer, the latter having been ordered by SAS as part of the co-operation that had developed between the two companies. Swissair went on to add further DC-8s to replace the DC-6Bs and DC-7Cs, receiving a series-50 aircraft in October 1963 and seven DC-8-62/CFs between November 1967 and February 1970. The Caravelle fleet peaked at nine aircraft in February 1964, although following the introduction of Douglas DC-9-15s (and later DC-9-30s) the type was relegated to less prestigious routes and phased out altogether by the summer of 1971. Another type that assisted in replacing the earlier piston-engined aircraft was the Convair 990A 'Coronado', eight of which were delivered to Swissair from early 1962 (including two leased to SAS). Prior to the introduction of these aircraft the airline leased two Convair 880s, between August 1961 and May 1962. A long standing relationship with the Douglas DC-9 began with the delivery of five series-15 aircraft from July 1967, although none of these remained in use beyond September 1968 following the subsequent introduction of DC-9-30s, which had started to arrive from October of the previous year. Major expansion followed the introduction of wide-bodied Boeing 747s and Douglas DC-10-30s from January 1971 and November 1972 respectively, as Swissair's international network developed into a truly world-wide system of scheduled passenger and freight routes.

Up until the introduction of the brown and black cheatline arrangement in use today, Swissair's livery had been based on the national colours of red and white - with the Swiss flag taking pride of the place on the fin. While this remained the standard colouring of the company for many years, its application often varied between different types - as illustrated by Convair 440 HB-LMN and Cv-990A 'Coronado' HB-ICH. Another variation, adopted by the Caravelles, involved extending the Swiss flag to the base of the fin (due to the awkward positioning of the horizontal stabilisers), while on the first Boeing 747s the anti-dazzle shield was extended over the cockpit windows in a somewhat unique fashion.

TAP (TRANSPORTES AEREOS PORTUGUESES)

TAP was formed by the Secretariate of Civil Aeronautics in 1944 and commenced regular scheduled operations on September 19th 1946 using a fleet of war surplus Douglas DC-3s, initially between Lisbon and Madrid. Several months after the inaugural flight a second regular service was opened between Lisbon and Lourenco Marques, linking Portugal with its major African colonies. Known as the 'Imperial Line', the service took six days to complete and routed via Casablanca, Villa Cisneros, Bathurst, Robertsville, Accra, Libreville, Luanda, Leopoldeville, Luluabourg, Elizabethville and Salisbury. Services to Paris and London were inaugurated in 1948 and '49 respectively, following the introduction of Douglas DC-4s. In 1953 TAP became a joint stock company and merged with Aero Portuguesa, which had operated services from Lisbon to Tangier and Casablanca. Major expansion followed and the original DC-3s and DC-4s were soon replaced by a modern fleet of Lockheed Super Constellations. These aircraft were used over TAP's entire network until the introduction of Caravelles in 1962, which entered service on mainline European services. By the summer of 1966 two Boeing 707s were in operation on routes to Africa, New York and Rio de Janeiro and with the introduction of three 727-100s in 1967 TAP phased out its remaining Constellations and became the first European carrier to operate an all-jet fleet, which was greatly expanded in subsequent years.

The livery illustrated by Boeing 707-382C CS-TBF was introduced by the first Super Constellations in 1955 and welcomed all new aircraft to the fleet, including Caravelles, Boeing 707s, 727-100s, 727-200s (from early 1975) and 747s (from early 1972), up until the current livery was introduced in 1979. In later years 'The Airline of Portugal' legend was added below the tail motif and the blue bird subsequently disappeared.

TRANSAIR SWEDEN

Transair Sweden was founded in 1950 as Nordisk Aerotransport and initially concentrated on newspaper and mail distribution. The name Transair was adopted the following year and in 1953 a Douglas DC-3 was added to the fleet as passenger and freight charters were developed. A fleet of Douglas DC-6 and Curtiss C-46 Commando aircraft was steadily built up during the following years, and additional DC-3s were also leased or purchased. Transair undertook flights on behalf of the United Nations during the Congo crisis and later reached a provisional agreement to conduct air services on behalf of the Congo Government, which led to the formation of Transair Congo in 1963. Inclusive tour charters, flown for Swedish, Danish, Swiss and German travel agencies, were mostly undertaken by the DC-6Bs, as were general passenger and freight charters - flown on a worldwide scale. The Curtiss Commandos operated freight services within Europe, including regular scheduled flights to Germany on behalf of SAS. Four of these aircraft were also operated by its African subsidiary, together with a DC-6. In 1965 the airline acquired nine ex-Eastern Douglas DC-7Bs to replace the DC-6 and DC-6B fleets, of which three and six respectively were employed. The airline went on to operate a total of eleven DC-7Bs following the purchase of two from South African Airways in March 1966, although by October 1969 the last of these had been withdrawn from use. During the winter of 1967/68 Transair took delivery of two new Boeing 727-100s, and later added a convertible -100C model in September 1968.

On October 1st 1969 the airline was merged with Scanair, the charter arm of SAS, and its aircraft were repainted to wear a combined Transair/Sunjet livery (as illustrated by 727-100C SE-DDC). Transair Sweden was fully absorbed by Scanair during the summer of 1981 and the Boeing 727s (of which four were now operated) were sold between August and September of that year, when the name and livery finally ceased to exist.

TAE (TRABAJOS AEREOS Y ENLACES S.A.)

TAE was created to serve the package holiday market and commenced operations in April 1967 from Palma de Mallorca. The original Douglas DC-7C (illustrated) was soon supplemented by another, and as business picked up the airline made arrangements to lease a third aircraft, which arrived in July 1968. By now, most of the airlines plying for business from Palma were using turboprop or jet equipment, and while the DC-7 had been a popular choice a few years earlier TAE's entry into the market came at a time when other companies were upgrading their fleets. Unable to compete on equal terms with its rivals, and without the necessary financing to modernise its fleet, TAE suspended operations during the summer of 1970 to re-organise.

New life was eventually breathed back into the airline three years later and with a new colour scheme (illustrated) and improved financial backing from Naviera Aznar S.A. (a local shipping company), TAE took to the air again during the summer of 1973 with two ex-UTA Douglas DC-8-30s. The airline's position improved following the collapse of Air Spain and in April 1975 a Caravelle 10B3 was leased from Sterling Airways of Denmark to supplement the DC-8s. A second was added a year later and a third in March 1979. Inclusive-tour flights were operated from Palma to all parts of Europe (especially Germany) and North Africa.

Once again, the age and poor economics of its fleet made TAE less favourable with the tour companies as time went on, and following a downturn in business the Caravelles were returned to Sterling during the winter of 1981 and the airline ceased to exist soon afterwards.

Transavia Holland, known until 1967 as Transavia (Limburg) NV, was founded in 1965 and began charter and inclusive tour operations on November 17th 1966 when the Dutch Dancing Theatre was flown to Naples. The initial fleet of two Douglas DC-6s and one DC-6B was increased to ten aircraft during the following year - with the addition of two DC-6As and five DC-6Bs (including four leased from Loftleidir). A leased Boeing 707-320C was also used between May and October 1968 on transatlantic charters, effectively marking the start of jet operations by the airline.

By 1969 most of Transavia's competitors in the charter and inclusive tour market were using jet equipment, so it leased two Caravelle 3s from Sud Aviation and disposed of its DC-6s, the last three leaving at the end of the 1969 summer season. It was later decided to standardise on the Caravelle, and so the airline purchased three series-3 aircraft from Swissair and six Caravelle 6Rs from United Airlines, to supplement and eventually replace those leased from the manufacturer. Boeing 707 operations were resumed in April 1970 (again with leased aircraft), and lasted until September 1971. The airline finally acquired its own '707, a series-120B, in March 1972, which it operated over the next ten years - supplemented between February 1976 and May 1977 by a leased 707-320C. The type was chiefly used on charters from Rotterdam to New York, Edmonton, Calgary, Toronto and Vancouver.

The Caravelle fleet continued to grow and by the summer of 1973 no less than twelve were in service, including two '6Ns purchased from Alitalia in April and May of that year. In addition to serving the needs of the tour operators, Transavia also discovered another revenue earning activity for its Caravelles, namely in flying them on behalf of other airlines. The company soon earned a reputation for being able to supply aircraft at short notice and was often called upon to airlift stranded passengers. Some of these contracts lasted a month or more, although the majority involved just one or two flights - usually to cover for an unserviceable aircraft or to save an airline's credibility in times of industrial unrest. The Caravelles were also chartered by some well known musicians who used them in support of European tours. These included pop idol David Cassidy (March 1973), The Osmonds (October-November 1973) and Frank Sinatra (May 1975). The withdrawal of the Caravelle fleet was brought forward by the oil crisis of the early 'seventies, which encouraged the airline to acquire more fuel efficient aircraft. Between May 1974 and May '75 the airline took delivery of seven Boeing 737-200s, including one leased from Britannia Airways and three from United. The airline also leased an Airbus A300B2 from the manufacturer between May 1976 and January 1977, but went on to standardise on the Boeing twinjet.

Douglas DC-6 PH-TRB illustrates the original 'T-bird' livery of Transavia, with two-tone green tail markings and the familiar black 'T' motif - missing from the fuselage on this occasion. The livery was also adopted by the original Boeing 707s and Caravelles, prior to the introduction of the design illustrated by 707-120B PH-TVA, which also coloured the '737 fleet in later years. The leased Airbus A300B2 had its own unique livery based on the standard green and black colouring but with changes made to the title and cheatline arrangements.

TRANS EUROPA

Trans Europa was formed in July 1965 to provide general passenger and cargo charters, and commenced flying in September of that year with a Douglas DC-7. Inclusive tour operations were introduced the following summer and between March and July 1966 the airline added two DC-7Cs and four DC-4s to its fleet. These services were flown from Palma and Las Palmas to destinations throughout Europe and North Africa. Another DC-7C was added in May 1967 and from then on the airline turned its attention towards jet aircraft.

Trans Europa ordered a total of three Caravelles from the manufacturer, two '11Rs and one '10R, in May and October 1969 respectively, and expanded its fleet with the addition of several used examples throughout the 'seventies. The two Caravelle 11Rs (EC-BRY illustrated) were delivered in July and September 1969 but went straight on lease to Iberia, and it was not until the following spring that holidaymakers sampled jet travel with Trans Europa for the first time, this being made possible by the arrival of the airline's ordered Caravelle 10R in March 1970. Trans Europa continued to operate just the one aircraft until Iberia returned the two '11Rs in 1972, by which time the Douglas DC-7s had been phased out. The following summer saw all three Caravelles engaged in the busy charter programmes from Palma and Las Palmas, with Trans Europa emerging as a major operator with an appetite for expansion. The purchase of a former LTU Caravelle 10R in February 1974 endorsed this growth and with the demise of Air Spain a year later the airline found itself with an even larger share of the market. The remaining DC-4s were withdrawn following the introduction of a former Alia Caravelle 10R in April 1975. Trans Europa eventually employed a fleet of seven Caravelles following the purchase of aircraft from Air Afrique and Iberia in June 1978 and March 1979 respectively, but like so many other airlines, particularly in Spain, it became a victim of rising fuel costs during the early 'eighties and eventually went out of business in 1982.

TMA - TRANS MEDITERRANEAN AIRWAYS

Trans Mediterranean Airways was formed in 1953 and commenced operations using two Avro York freighters on non-scheduled services, flying fresh produce to oil stations in the Arabian Gulf. On February 12th 1959 it became a joint stock company with a paid up capital of £L6 million and obtained Lebanese Government approval to operate regular scheduled freight services. This coincided with the expansion of the York fleet and the introduction of two Douglas DC-4s. However, the Yorks were soon replaced following the purchase of more DC-4s and DC-6A/Bs, the latter from March 1963. The network and fleet continued to be expanded during the years ahead, with initial routes connecting the Lebanon with Kuwait, Dhahran, Teheran, Doha, Bahrain, Kabul, as well as Basle, Frankfurt, and later London and Paris in Europe. By 1967 the fleet comprised six Douglas DC-6A/Bs and four DC-4s. A Lockheed L.100-20 Hercules was also leased from Pacific Western during the summer months, and in subsequent years the airline leased Canadair CL-44s from Seaboard World and Slick Airways to supplement its fleet. On April 14th 1971 TMA inaugurated the first round-the-world cargo service from Beirut to Karachi, Bombay, Bangkok, Singapore, Manila, Taipei, Osaka, Tokyo, Anchorage, New York, Amsterdam, Basle and Beirut, following the introduction of three leased Boeing 707-320Cs. The remaining DC-4s were phased out at around the same time, and with the introduction of additional '707-320Cs the DC-6s finally disappeared during the winter of 1973/74. The airline went on to add two Boeing 747-100F freighters from May 1975, but continuing troubles in the Lebanon made the long term operation of these aircraft impossible.

Douglas DC-6A/B OD-AEG illustrates TMA's livery in its original form, the yellow pyramid motif dating back to the days of Avro York operations; an updated version was also adopted by the first Boeing 707s. In later years it was decided to adopt green fuselage colouring and yellow 'TMA of Lebanon' titles, this design being synonymous to the '707 and '747 aircraft.

Transmeridian Air Cargo was originally founded as Trans Meridian Flying Services to operate long-range, ad-hoc cargo charters using two leased Douglas DC-4s. Operations commenced from Liverpool on December 15th 1962 and in May of the following year the airline won a contract from the Ministry of Defence to operate cargo flights from Lyneham and Manston to points in Europe and the Middle East. This work was later extended to the Far East following the introduction of a Douglas DC-7C in December 1964, and the DC-4s were returned to Trans World Leasing. The longer range of this aircraft complimented the airline's activities and with the introduction of a second DC-7C in early 1966 the company moved its operations to Luton Airport and focused on charters to the Middle and Far East, and Africa. Altogether, five Douglas DC-7Cs were acquired by Trans Meridian but no more than three were operated at any one time. The aircraft illustrated, G-AWBI, was used between January 1968 and April 1969 and was the last of the five to be acquired. The company moved operations to Cambridge in 1967 and finally settled in at Stansted during the following summer, where it established its own maintenance facility in a quite corner of the airfield. The new name of Trans Meridian (London) Ltd. was also adopted.

By now Trans Meridian was looking to replace the DC-7Cs with turboprop equipment, while at the same time Flying Tigers was planning to offload some of its Canadair CL-44 swingtails following the introduction of Super DC-8 freighters. Two of these aircraft were purchased and arrived at Stansted in early 1969, and by April the remaining DC-7s had been sold. The airline acquired a third CL-44 towards the end of the year and added a fourth for the summer of 1970, by which time it had changed its name to Transmeridian Air Cargo (TAC). The CL-44s also introduced a new livery based on the natural metal finish of Flying Tigers with red and black cheatlines and tail markings. A white 'K' was also added to the design in recognition of Mr. T.D. Keegan, who had a controlling interest in TAC and later went on to acquire British Air Ferries as well. In the summer of 1970 the company purchased a former Flying Tigers CL-44 that had been converted by the Conroy Aircraft Company for the carriage of outsized cargo. Registered N447T, it joined the fleet in July and was affectionately known as 'Skymonster'. TAC went on to add another four ex-Flying Tigers CL-44s during the winter of 1971/72, thereby increasing its fleet of the type to nine - including the Conroy conversion.

In addition to charter activities, the CL-44s also operated scheduled services from Stansted to Africa and the Far East. The 'Ghengis Khan' route originated from any of four European terminals (Stansted, Basle, Ostend and Rotterdam) and connected with Istanbul, Nicosia, Kuwait, Bahrain, Abu Dhabi, Karachi, Delhi, Bombay, Bangkok, Hong Kong, Singapore and Jakarta. Another service linked Stansted with Cairo and Asmara while the 'Impala' route was flown regularly between Stansted, Kano and Lagos. In late 1975 one of the CL-44s was painted in the colours of Limburg Air Cargo and operated a weekly service between Maastricht and Hong Kong.

Jet operations started during the summer of 1977 following the purchase of two Douglas DC-8-54Fs, by which time the livery illustrated by the 'Skymonster' had been introduced. Some two years later, on August 15th 1979, Transmeridian Air Cargo merged with Gatwick-based IAS to form the short-lived British Cargo Airlines.

TIA (TRANS INTERNATIONAL AIRLINES)

Trans International Airlines was formed in 1948 as Los Angeles Air Service and began operations that same year, quickly expanding its activities as a US intra-state and contract carrier, specialising in military charter work; the subsequent name being adopted in July 1960. Two years later the airline became a wholly-owned subsidiary of the Studebaker Corporation, but reverted to independent ownership in 1964. Based at McCarran Field, Las Vegas, the airline operated three Lockheed L-1049H Super Constellations and one L-1049G, and had also introduced two Douglas DC-8-50s for MATS charter work across the Pacific. In 1968 ownership was sold to the Transamerica Corporation and a move to Oakland (California) followed. This also coincided with the delivery of two new Boeing 727-100Cs, while seven Douglas DC-8-63CFs were ordered for delivery between November 1968 and May 1970. In the years that followed passenger charter services were developed throughout the United States, and to Europe, Africa, the Caribbean, Asia, the South Pacific, the Far East and Central and South America. The DC-8s were joined by three DC-10-30CFs during the summer of 1973 and the company later ordered five Boeing 747-200Cs for delivery from December 1979, by which time it claimed to be the largest vacation charter airline in the world.

The livery illustrated by Douglas DC-10-30 N102TV was changed in April 1976 to link the company more closely with its parent, and the name Transamerica Airlines was also adopted. In December 1976 the airline merged with Saturn Airways, whose activities included principally commercial cargo and military charters, and its fleet of Lockheed Hercules and Electra freighters were soon repainted to wear the new Transamerica livery. The Boeing 747-200C order was later reduced to three aircraft, while the DC-8s were converted to series-73 standard and the DC-10s were sold. Transamerica Airlines eventually ceased operations on September 30th 1986.

TRANSPORT FLUG

Transport Flug commenced operations during the summer of 1965 using an ex-Interocean Douglas DC-4, operating ad-hoc and contract freight charters, mostly on behalf of other airlines (especially Lufthansa). The fleet was soon increased and by August 1967 three DC-4s were in operation. However, there were still times when additional capacity was needed, such as during 1968 when the daily Lufthansa cargo service between Frankfurt and Manchester was sub-contracted to Aer Turas; the reason for this being that one of the DC-4s had been assigned to Alitalia on a full time basis. However, this problem was later solved on March 31st 1969 when Transport Flug merged with Allgemeine Lufttransport (All-Air), which had also operated three Douglas DC-4s. The airline also acquired two ex-Germanair Douglas DC-6As, but following the introduction of 'quick-change' Boeing 737-200Cs by Lufthansa (from December 1969) many of the contracts were terminated and Transport Flug ceased operations shortly afterwards.

The standard black and white colouring of Transport Flug is illustrated by Douglas DC-4 D-ACAB, which is seen at Frankfurt in the spring of 1970 alongside a Seaboard World Curtiss Commando. The Douglas DC-6As retained the red and black cheatline arrangement of Germanair although black 'TF' initials were displayed on the fin and the word 'Cargo' appeared on the cabin roof.

TWA's history goes back to 1925 when the first of its parental foursome, Western Air Express, bid for a mail contract covering the Los Angeles-Salt Lake City route, the first service being inaugurated on April 17th 1926. In 1930 W.A.E. purchased Standard Airlines (later sold to American Airways), which had operated a passenger service between Los Angeles and El Paso since 1927, and on July 16th joined with Transcontinental Air Transport-Maddux Airlines to became Transcontinental and Western Air (TWA). T.A.T. was organised in 1928 and operated a combined rail-air route from New York to Los Angeles from July 7th 1929. A year later T.A.T. gained control of Maddux Airlines, which was founded in 1927.

TWA developed its domestic trunk routes and was instrumental in the design of such famous aircraft as the Douglas DC-1, DC-2, DC-3, the Boeing Stratoliner and the Lockheed Constellation, with which the airline inaugurated its first overseas flight (from Washington to Paris) on December 5th 1945. Regular international services followed from February 5th 1946, and on May 17th 1950 the company's title was appropriately changed to Trans World Airlines Inc.

TWA went on to acquire and operate more Lockheed Constellations than any other airline in the world, constantly adding newer and improved models as they became available. The original L-049/749s were joined by L-749As (from March 1950), L-1049s (from May 1952), L-1049Gs (from March 1955), L-1049Hs (from March 1958) and L-1649A Starliners (from May 1957). With the Starliners, TWA introduced non-stop services from New York to Europe and also a new non-stop service over the pole from Los Angeles and San Francisco to London. However, the advantages of operating these aircraft soon disappeared with the arrival of the first turbojet Boeing 707s, which TWA introduced on non-stop services between New York and California and on routes between New York, London and European points from 1959. However, some of the Starliners continued to haul freight over the Atlantic until 1963, with as many as twelve aircraft converted for such operations. In addition to the types already mentioned, the airline also used a large fleet of Martin 202 and 404 aircraft on domestic services from July 1950 and November 1951 respectively, most of which were phased out by or during the early 'sixties.

With the advent of the jet age TWA found itself with well over one hundred Constellations/Starliners to replace, a 1959 count revealing more than seventy L-049/749/749As alone. That same year the airline took delivery of fifteen Boeing 707-120s and four 707-320s, and while these aircraft were ideal for the transcontinental and coast-to-coast flights the airline was still faced with the problem of replacing its piston-engined fleet domestically, especially as it had chosen to neglect any turboprop alternatives. Although this problem was partly solved by the introduction of Convair 880s and Boeing 727-100s from February 1961 and April 1964 respectively, it still left many routes operated by the Constellations. In September 1961 the airline ordered twenty Caravelle 10As (plus fifteen options) for delivery in 1963, but then decided to cancel these in favour of the Douglas DC-9. TWA eventually took delivery of twenty DC-9-14s from February 1966 to replace the remaining Constellations, the airline's last piston-engined passenger service being flown by an L-749A as late as April 6th 1967! The Boeing 707 fleet was expanded from 1960 and by 1965 eighty of these were either in service or on order, including -120, -120B, -320, -320B and -320C models. The 727-100s were later supplemented by series -200 aircraft (from March 1968), while the Convair 880s were phased out between 1973/74 following the introduction of Lockheed TriStars. TWA originally entered the wide bodied era on the last day of 1969 when, on December 31st, it took delivery of the first of many Boeing 747-100s - named 'City of Paris'.

Lockheed L.1649A Starliner N7301C and Boeing 707-320B N8733 illustrate two classic TWA liveries, the 'twin globe' design remaining in use for some seventeen years - prior to the unveiling of the present design on November 30th 1974.

TUNIS AIR

Tunis Air was formed in 1948 as a branch airline of Air France, with the participation of the Tunisian Government and other private interests. Operations began in 1949 with Douglas DC-3s over a small local network previously served by the French national airline, and this was followed by regional routes to Casablanca, Tripoli, and Ghadames, a vital oasis on the borders of Libya, Tunisia and Algeria. A European service to Paris via Marseilles and Nice was inaugurated with DC-4s in 1953, and by 1965 had been extended to Switzerland and Italy.

Jet operations were initiated in September 1961 following the introduction of a Caravelle 3 on the Tunis-Paris route, but most other destinations continued to be served by DC-3 and DC-4 equipment for several more years. A second Caravelle was added in March 1964, followed by another in March 1966 and finally a fourth in February 1968, and as each new aircraft arrived so the network was expanded. Tunis Air also took delivery of a new Nord 262A in April 1969 to replace Douglas DC-3 equipment on local services.

Between February 1972 and June 1977 the airline took delivery of ten new Boeing 727-200s, with the last four effectively replacing the Caravelle fleet. With these aircraft came the livery illustrated by Caravelle 3 TS-TAR, which in later years was also applied to Boeing 737-200s (from October 1979) and an Airbus A300B4 (delivered in May 1982). The tail motif was previously based on the crescent and star combination of the Tunisian flag, from where the red and white colouring also originates.

TURKISH AIRLINES (TURK HAVA YOLLARI)

Turkish Airlines was set up under the Ministry of National Defence on May 20th 1933 and was known as Devlet Hava Yollari (Turkish State Airlines) until February 20th 1956, when the airline became an independent corporation. DHY inaugurated a thrice-weekly service in 1933 between the country's two major cities - Istanbul and Ankara (via Eskisehir), using de Havilland Rapides. The airline initially concentrated on establishing domestic links, but international expansion began in 1947 with the opening of a route to Athens, followed in 1950 by services to Nicosia, Beirut and Cairo. The Rapides were later replaced by de Havilland Herons, while Douglas DC-3s (operated from 1946) were supplemented and eventually replaced by a mix of turboprop Fokker and Fairchild F-27s. Services to London and Brussels were inaugurated in 1958 following the introduction of five Vickers Viscount 700s.

In August 1967 the airline leased a Douglas DC-9-15 from the manufacturer to gain experience with the type, which also marked the start of jet operations. Ten Douglas DC-9-30s were subsequently introduced (initially at a rate of two a year) from the summer of 1968, as the route network began to spread across Europe and the Middle East. The airline also ordered three Boeing 727-200s for delivery in November 1971, but cancelled these following the introduction of three ex-Pan Am Boeing 707-320s earlier that year. The '707 fleet was later standardised on the model -120B (between 1974 and 1977), the -320B (between 1978 and 1985) and the -320C (from 1981). During the winter of 1972/73 the airline introduced three Douglas DC-10-10s, and in doing so became the first operator of the type in Europe. At around the same time the first of five ordered Fokker F.28-1000s arrived to replace turboprop F.27s, and with the introduction of Boeing 727-200s from November 1974, three years later than originally planned, the fleet composition was complete.

The livery illustrated by DC-10-10 TC-JAV was used by Turkish Airlines for many years and originated during the post-DHY era. However, the original Boeing 707s adopted a solid red cheatline and tail band, similar in many ways to the design in use today

United Airlines was formed on July 1st 1931 as the management company for Boeing Air Transport, National Air Transport, Pacific Air Transport and Varney Air Lines, and became operational on July 20th 1934. The oldest of these, Varney Air Lines, was bought out of the company again in 1934, and later became Continental Airlines. Building on the existing routes of its predecessors, United established a comprehensive coast-to-coast network which was extended to Hawaii in 1947

Throughout its history United has been responsible for many 'firsts', including the introduction of the twin-engined Boeing 247 in 1933, the Douglas DC-6 'Mainliner' in April 1947, and in later years the Douglas DC-8, Boeing 720, Caravelle 6R, Boeing 727, 737-200 and Douglas DC-10. One of the most significant developments in the airline's post war history was the purchase, on June 1st 1961, of Capital Airlines, in what was at the time the biggest ever airline merger.

United Airlines entered the jet age on September 18th 1959 when it introduced Douglas DC-8-10s on the New York-San Francisco service, while Boeing 720 operations began in July 1960. On February 25th 1960 the airline became the first customer for the Caravelle 6R, ordering twenty aircraft (plus twenty options) for delivery from May 1961. It entered service on the New York to Chicago run on July 14th, to coincide with French national day, and for three years United enjoyed pitching these jets against the piston and turboprop aircraft of its competitors. Due to the launching of the Boeing 727 the airline failed to confirm its twenty options, but the initial Caravelles remained in use until the early 'seventies when they were finally ousted by the more fuel efficient Boeing 737s.

By 1965, United's fleet comprised thirty-eight Douglas DC-8-20/50s (plus ten -50s on order), three DC-8F-50s (plus three on order), twenty-nine Boeing 720s, twenty-eight 727-100s (plus eighty two -100/200s on order), twenty Caravelle 6Rs, twenty-three Douglas DC-7s, six DC-7Fs, thirty DC-6s, seven DC-6As, forty DC-6Bs, seventeen Convair 340s and forty-five Viscount 700s. Most of the DC-6s were replaced with the introduction of additional Boeing 727s, including 727-100Cs (from March 1967) and 727-200s (from May 1968). United began '727 services between Denver and San Francisco on February 6th 1964, and introduced the type to nationwide routes mid-year. Douglas DC-8-61s entered service from November 1966, representing another 'first' for the airline, and by June 1969 thirty of these high capacity airliners had been delivered. United was the second customer for the Boeing 737 (after Lufthansa), but the first to order the -200 model, which had been developed specifically for 'local service' operations. The type entered service in January 1968 and within two years seventy-five of these aircraft were either in service or on order. The airline went on to add Boeing 747-100s (from June 1970) and Douglas DC-10-10s (from July 1971), and eventually built up a fleet of over 400 jet aircraft

Douglas DC-6 N37536 is seen at San Francisco in June 1958 during the changeover of liveries - note the aircraft in the background wearing the subsequent livery (also illustrated by Boeing 727-100 N7204U - at the same location twenty years later). This was later replaced by the current 'double U' scheme in 1974, first unveiled by DC-8-20 N8031U on June 17th of that year, although it took many years for this to be adopted fleetwide.

UTA (UNION DE TRANSPORT AERIENS)

UTA was formed on October 1st 1963 through the merger of Union Aeromaritime de Transport (UAT) - see separate entry, and Compagnie de Transport Aeriens Intercontinentaux (TAI). The latter was formed in association with the Messagenes Maritime Shipping Company in June 1946 as a charter company and started operations a month later. Scheduled services followed in 1948 to Africa (chiefly Madagascar) and to the Far East, and in 1956 TAI took over the Air France routes to Australia and New Caledonia. These were later extended to New Zealand and via Polynesia and Honolulu to Los Angeles, connecting with Air France Boeing 707 services to Paris (via Montreal).

UTA built on the experience and routes of these major French airlines, inheriting a fleet of six Douglas DC-8-30s, eight DC-6Bs, two DC-6As, two DC-4s and a Beech 18. In 1965 UTA ordered two Caravelle10Rs for its medium range routes, receiving the first of these in January of the following year. One of these aircraft was based at Noumea and operated services to the New Hebrides, Wallis Island and Auckland, while the other, based in Paris, flew the Le Bourget-Marseilles-Las Palmas-Bamako-Bobo Dioulasso run and later the Le Bourget-Marseilles-Tripoli service, until replaced by DC-8s in 1973. The following year UTA acquired two Fairchild F-27As from Hughes Airwest for its regional network and the remaining Caravelle was leased to Air Afrique and later sold to the French Air Force.

Two of the original DC-8-30s were converted to series-50 standard during the summer of 1965 and towards the end of the year the airline added two new DC-8-50s (including one series-55F). The Douglas DC-6 fleet started to be phased out at around the same time, with two going to the French Air Force and another to Iran Air. Other DC-6s were transferred to Aeromaritime, which was created by UTA in 1966 to operate passenger and freight charter services. UTA continued to expand its DC-8 fleet, taking delivery of four new DC-8-62s (between February 1968 and May 1969), two ex-Eastern DC-8-63PFs (in April 1973 and February 1974) and three used DC-8-55Fs (from August 1970). The airline also ordered five Douglas DC-10-30s (later increased to six) for delivery from February 1973, and went on to acquire various passenger/freight models of the Boeing 747, with the first joining the fleet in September 1978.

The liveries illustrated by Douglas DC-6B F-BGSL and DC-8-62 F-BNLE were synonymous to those types, the Caravelles adopting a totally different scheme featuring a winged 'UTA' tail motif in blue and green. The modern day scheme was introduced by the first DC-10s and DC-8-63s from 1973, and brought a common image to the fleet for the first time. One DC-8-63 was, however, operated in the earlier livery, the aircraft being leased from CP Air for a period of twelve months from March 1972.

UAT (UNION AEROMARITIME DE TRANSPORT)

UAT was formed in November 1949 in association with Air France, SATA, and the shipping line Cie Maritime des Chargeurs Reunis, and developed routes to French Equatorial Africa, to Rhodesia, Mozambique, South Africa, and subsequently to many other African territories as well as to the Middle and Far East. Douglas DC-4 services linked Paris with Dakar, Pointe Noire and Saigon by the start of the 'fifties, and during 1951 the Dakar service was extended to Abidjan. Three Douglas DC-3s were acquired in 1952 to operate feeder services from Douala, and experiments were conducted with these aircraft using auxiliary jet power to enhance performance. On December 11th 1952 UAT took delivery of the first of three ordered de Havilland Comet 1As, narrowly beating Air France in inaugurating the first jet services from Paris. One of these aircraft was lost at Dakar in June 1953, while the others were withdrawn from use in April 1954 and replaced by two Douglas DC-6Bs. The airline had already acquired two DC-6As from Slick Airways several months earlier, and following a merger with Aigle Azur another three DC-6Bs were absorbed in May 1955. In the meantime the African-based DC-3s were replaced by de Havilland Herons. The airline went on to acquire another four DC-6Bs between March 1958 and June 1959 and later resumed jet operations following the delivery of two new Douglas DC-8-30s from June 1960, with a used aircraft being added in October 1962. UAT also participated with Air France in the creation of Air Afrique, and provided it with equipment.

Douglas DC-6B F-BGTX illustrates the full blue and yellow colouring used by UAT until October 1963, when the airline merged with TAI (Transports Aeriens Intercontinentaux) to form UTA.

VARIG

Varig was organised with Brasilian capital on May 7th 1927 and began operations on February 3rd 1928 with a single Dornier Wal over the Porto Alegre-Rio Grande route, taken over from the Kondor Syndikat. In 1951 Varig acquired Aerea Geral, a domestic operator, and then became the largest airline in South America in August 1961 when it took over the REAL consortium and absorbed its fleet and routes. On February 9th 1965 Panair do Brasil was grounded by by decree of the Brasilian President with debts exceeding $60 million, and its international routes were immediately transferred to Varig, with domestic services being shared between Cruzeiro and VASP. At the time of its collapse, Panair operated three Douglas DC-8-30s, three Caravelle 6Rs, two Douglas DC-7s, ten Lockheed L-049 Constellations and five Catalina Flying boats. Varig absorbed the DC-8s into its fleet, which at the time comprised three Convair 990As (delivered in March 1963), two Boeing 707-420s (delivered in June 1960), five Lockheed L-1049Gs (delivered from May 1955 - PP-VDE illustrated), four L-1049Hs (inherited from REAL), five L.188 Electras (acquired to replace Caravelle 3s in service from September 1959), five Douglas DC-6Bs, one Convair 440, ten Convair 340s, twenty-two Curtiss C-46 Commandos and forty DC-3s. Varig's international route network already served Montevideo, Buenos Aires, Bogota, Panama City, Mexico City, Los Angeles (via Lima), New York and Miami (via Caracas and Santo Domingo), the most significant gain from Panair being its long established routes to Europe.

Through all its take overs Varig had acquired a large and varied fleet that needed to be modernised in some areas and standardised in others. Although some of the older DC-3s etc. remained in use for several more years, the fleet was mainly shaped around the Lockheed Electra and Boeing 707-320C (from December 1966), joined by the 727-100 (from October 1970) and 737-200 (from October 1974).

WARDAIR CANADA

Wardair was formed in 1952 to continue the activities of the Polaris Charter Company, which had been founded by Maxwell Ward at Yellowknife in 1946 to support mining operations in the Northwest Territories. Operations started on June 6th 1953 with a de Havilland Otter and were mainly confined to the Arctic regions of Canada until 1962, when the airline entered the lucrative transatlantic charter market using a Douglas DC-6B leased from Canadian Pacific Airlines. At the same time the name of the company was changed to Wardair Canada Ltd.

The airline purchased its own DC-6B from KLM in March 1963, although this was later leased to Pacific Western following the delivery of a new Boeing 727-100 in April 1966, which assumed most of the transatlantic charter flights. DC-6 operations finally came to an end in April 1968, when Wardair introduced the first of two Boeing 707-320Cs (CF-FAN illustrated). In 1965 domestic services were flown by three Otters, one Beaver, one Beech 18 and a Bristol 170 Freighter, although as time went on the airline re-equipped with Twin Otter and eventually Dash 7 aircraft. The transatlantic operations were given a further boost in April 1973 when Wardair received its first Boeing 747-100, after which the '727 was phased out and sold. A second '747 arrived in December 1974 and the two 707-320Cs were finally ousted by two 747-200Bs and two Douglas DC-10-30s, delivered from June and December 1978 respectively. The DC-10 fleet was later increased to three following the purchase of a former Singapore Airlines aircraft in September 1981.

Wardair Canada was absorbed by Canadian Airlines International on October 16th 1989, by which time its fleet had been standardised on Airbus Industrie A310-300 equipment.

WESTERN AIRLINES

Western Airlines claimed to be America's oldest continuously-operated airline, tracing its history back to the formation of Sacramento-based Western Air Express on July 13th 1925, which inaugurated mail services between Los Angeles and Salt Lake City on April 17th 1926 using a Douglas M-2 open cockpit biplane; followed by the first passenger flights on May 23rd. After the amalgamation with T.A.T. to form Transcontinental and Western Airlines (TWA) on July 16th 1930, Western Air Express continued as a separate entity, and for a while operated under the name of General Airlines; the name Western Airlines being adopted on March 11th 1941. The airline extended its route system in the early years through the acquisition of many smaller companies, including National Parks Airways (August 1937) and Inland Air (October 1943).

By the start of 1965 the airline operated over 9,500 miles of routes in the western and mid-western states, flying as far east as Minneapolis/St. Paul, northwards across the Canadian border to Calgary and southwards to Mexico. The fleet at the time comprised thirteen Boeing 720Bs (delivered from April 1961), twelve Lockheed L.188A Electras (delivered between May 1959 and February 1961), and fourteen Douglas DC-6Bs, which were in the process of being phased out. A further fourteen Boeing 720Bs were added between March 1965 and September 1967, and following the purchase of Pacific Northern Airlines on July 1st 1967 new routes were also opened to Alaska. Further expansion followed in 1968 when the airline took delivery of twenty-two new Boeing jets (five 707-320Cs and seventeen 737-200s), which also marked the end of passenger operations by the Electras. The airline went on to add more '737s, as well as 727-200s (from October 1969) and Douglas DC-10-10 'Spaceships' (from April 1973).

The livery illustrated by L.188A Electra N7135C was used until late 1970 when the modern DC-10-style scheme was introduced. The Indian head motif was used to substantiate Western's claim of being America's oldest airline - the indians being the original inhabitants. Western Airlines ceased to exist on April 1st 1987 following a merger with Delta Air Lines.

WORLD AIRWAYS

World Airways was formed in 1948 and commenced operations that same year using two Curtiss C-46 Commandos. The airline's initial business consisted mostly of military contract work, although some commercial charter flights were undertaken on an ad-hoc basis. From these humble beginnings, World Airways went on to become one of the world's leading non-scheduled airlines, due in no small part to Edward J. Daly, who rescued the company from its debts in 1960 and initiated major expansion. As significant to World was the advent of the Boeing 707-320C, the first of these being delivered in July 1963, which enabled the airline to extend its areas of operation and enter properly into the field of international commercial charter. World initially received three Boeing 707-320Cs during the summer of 1963 to replace four Lockheed Starliners, which had been leased from Lufthansa since mid-1962 to operate MATS charters from the US west coast to such destinations as Bangkok, Tokyo, Okinawa and Manila. As more of these aircraft were delivered from October 1965 so leased L-1049H Super Constellations were also returned to their owners, the '707 fleet finally peaking at eight aircraft in November 1967. That summer, the airline also took delivery of six new Boeing 727-100Cs to replace Douglas DC-6A/Bs used on US intra-state services. In addition to the long-haul military contract charters, the airline also initiated worldwide passenger and cargo charter operations, including a programme of transatlantic holiday charters to the United Kingdom and Europe. The Boeing 707s were effectively replaced by six Douglas DC-8-63CFs (introduced from March 1971), although some of these remained under World ownership for several years in support of the airline's leasing activities.

Further expansion followed in April 1973 when the airline took delivery of the first of three ordered Boeing 747-200Cs (N747WA illustrated), and from March 1978 World began to receive its first Douglas DC-10-30CFs - on which the fleet would be standardised in later years. With these aircraft came a modified livery, which basically added gold colouring to the existing design.

ZAMBIA AIRWAYS

Zambia Airways was formed in 1963 as a subsidiary of the Central African Airways Corporation to take over that company's operations in the newly independent state of Zambia (formerly known as Northern Rhodesia). Operations commenced on July 1st 1964 with two Douglas DC-3s and three DHC-2 Beavers. Two BAC 1-11-200s were introduced in early 1968 to open international services to East Africa, Kinshasa and Malawi, with flights to Europe following in 1970 with a leased Alitalia Douglas DC-8-43. Also that year, the airline took delivery of three Hawker Siddeley '748s to modernise domestic operations. These were now flown from Lusaka to several internal locations, including Kitwe and Ndola in the copperbelt region, Mansa, Kasama, Mbala and Kasaba Bay in the Sumbu National Park and Lake Tanganyika areas, Mfuwe and Chipata in the Luangwa Valley, Ngoma in the Kafue National Park and Livingstone by the spectacular Victoria Falls.

In March 1975 the airline entered into an agreement with Aer Lingus which involved the purchase of a Boeing 707-320C and the lease of 737-200. During the same month the two 1-11-200s were sold to Dan Air and a new livery was introduced to replace the design illustrated by '748 9J-ADM. The cheatline colours of orange, black, green and red were retained for their traditional values; orange - representing copper, Zambia's main export, black - representing the people, green - the fertile country and red - the blood of the people, with the most significant change being made to the tail colouring. The new livery was adopted by all aircraft with the exception of the leased DC-8-43, which returned to Alitalia at the end of the year to allow the international fleet to be standardised on the 707-320C. Another three of these aircraft were added to expand both passenger and freight services to Europe and Asia, while a new 737-200 was delivered in June 1976 to replace the leased Aer Lingus machine.

INDEX